SYMPTOMATIC: LIFE OF A SICKLE CELL CARRIER

AN INVISIBLE DISABILITY

MY STORY

LOUISE RACHAEL MWAPE MILLER

DISCLAIMER:

The views and opinions expressed within this book are the author's own personal experiences and are intended to prompt the reader to make informed decisions about their health. These should not be used as a substitute for treatment by or the advice of a professional health-care provider. The author and publisher will not be deemed responsible for any loss or damage of any kind suffered as a result of complete reliance of this book's contents or any errors or omissions herein.

Please note that the web addresses or links contained within this book may have changed since publication and may no longer be valid, due to the ever-evolving nature of the internet.

No part of this book may be reproduced in any form or by any electronic or mechanical means, including information storage and retrieval systems, without written permission from the author, except for the use of brief quotations in a book review.

Copyright © 2021 Louise Rachael Mwape Miller
First Published 2021 by JLG Publishing
www.jlgpublishing.com
Cover illustrations by Florence Packer
All rights reserved.
ISBN: 978-1-914442-07-0

DEDICATION

To all those warriors who are symptomatic carriers of sickle cell anaemia, known as having sickle cell trait, wherever you are based. Because I have felt your pain and walked in your shoes, I understand the importance of how necessary spreading awareness and telling my story is now! I hope this book encourages anybody who chooses to journey with me through the pages of some of the most painful parts of my life, that no matter what, life is a challenge and I may be a sickle cell trait warrior, but you are a warrior, because you are living in this battlefield called life! Keep pressing on and know that you are not alone! Even when it hurts to keep moving, lean forward and take the lessons and pain as a reason to push towards your purpose. You never know who is watching and who's life you might just save!

'For I know the plans and thoughts that I have for you,' says the Lord, 'plans for peace and well-being and not for disaster to give you a future and a hope.'

Jeremiah 29:11 (AMP)

FOREWORD

It is often said, 'Experience is the best teacher'; therefore, the awareness and understanding of certain events in life can be better communicated to the world by those who experienced the event. This applies to the sickle cell experiences of those with sickle cell traits by the author.

What we have always known about sickle cell disorder, in the past, is that sickle cell carriers (those with sickle cell traits – Haemoglobin AS or AC) hardly experience the sickle cell crises and sickle cell complications that those with sickle cell anaemia (Haemoglobin SS, SC or other variants) do experience. There has been scanty information in the medical community about sickle cell trait because of this which has affected the allocation of healthcare resources and approach of healthcare delivery to those with sickle cell traits.

Generally, there are many things about sickle cell disorder that the world does not know, this is more complicated for sickle cell carriers whom the medical community and the world have assumed they do not encounter the same challenges of those with sickle cell anaemia. As a medical doctor, I have never experienced a sickle cell carrier presenting with sickle cell crises and complications like those with sickle cell anaemia during my years of medical practice.

I eulogize the courage, tenacity, persistence, and doggedness of the author to make her voice of pains and unpleasantness from sickle cell trait heard by the medical community and the world. Her interaction with other sickle cell carriers validated her claim that people with sickle cell traits also experience sickle cell crises and complications. Even when no one was willing to listen, she kept talking, shouting, and crying to express herself and describe the true picture of sickle cell traits that the world has neglected for long. Her perseverance reminds me of the parable of Jesus Christ in ***Luke chapter 18*** about the widow who persistently voiced her problem to the king till she got justice.

The author has diligently taken time to describe her sickle cell experiences of sickle cell crises, sickle cell complications, sickle cell abuse and sickle cell stigmatization through her well-articulated stories and soul-searching poems.

Through this book, I can say finally, the medical community and world will listen to Mwape! The medical community and world will listen to all sickle cell carriers! The medical community and world will listen to all sickle cell warriors!

Dr. David Owoeye
Sickle Cell Warrior and Author
Infection Prevention and Control Specialist.

CONTENTS

ACKNOWLEDGMENTS

To my King Jesus who gave me His life, so I could fight the good fight for mine and entrusted me with a mission so big, I could only hope to fulfill it in this lifetime! Thank You Lord for carrying me through and for it all. I now live for You, because You died for me!

"For God so [greatly] loved and dearly prized the world, that He [even] gave His [One and] only begotten Son, so that whoever believes and trusts in Him [as Saviour] shall not perish but have eternal life."
John 3:16 (AMP)

To my African Queen, my beautiful and selfless mother, who has been there for me and literally, physically carried me every step of the way, no matter how heavy or painful the burden, even when it nearly cost you your life! No words could ever express the gratitude I have for you being my greatest gift on earth, thank you mama! I love you beyond measure!

'An excellent woman [one who is spiritual, capable, intelligent, and virtuous], who is he who can find her? .....
........Her children rise up and call her blessed (happy, prosperous, to be admired);'
Proverbs 31:10, 28 (AMP)

Thank you to Dr David Owoeye, thank you sir for finding the group and being a comfort and an encouragement to all of us sickle cell warriors, within our Facebook support group. I appreciate your time spent checking on my health and praying for my healing, as you were battling with your own health. I appreciate your insight and your faithfulness in spreading awareness of sickle cell and in being such a support to our fellow warriors across the sickle cell disorder spectrum. Thank you for lending your wisdom and medical experience and vast knowledge and sharing your personal experiences to benefit us all! I salute you and may God bless you and your family always! Without your book, "A Life With Sickle Cell Anaemia", I would be too afraid to have written mine, as a symptomatic Sickle Cell Trait Warrior!

May Sickle Cell Trait be recognized as a very real condition to all who present like they have the full-blown disorder! May we be taken seriously, so it prevents another life being taken prematurely or needlessly. May we be listened to and heard by those we run to for help in desperation! May research and funding be provided for all with Sickle Cell Disorder across the whole spectrum! Our lives matter too!

'.... Listen carefully......" Be not afraid nor dismayed.... for the battle is not yours, but God's!"
2 Chronicles 20:15b (AMP)

To my amazing graphics designer Florence, thank you for your patience and for going above and beyond my expectations in creating such a perfect cover to suit this book! Your skills and talent always exceed my expectations and I am so grateful we met all those years ago when I was looking for a graphics designer on the coach trip back to Leeds! Thank You for making this book happen!

To Jenica Leah, I am grateful for your time connecting with me as a fellow sickle cell warrior and for your professional guidance. Thank you for understanding why this book is so important. I'm so grateful to you that you listened and heard my story and you have become a major part of my newfound mission and goal! I am so grateful to be under the umbrella of JLG Publishing and inspired by such an amazing, strong and talented young woman! I am proud to have you in my support network as a sister warrior!

Finally, thank you to the reader who has taken the time out to purchase this book and find out more about this invisible condition, which has caused me and many others like me, to live like we have a disability, some from their childhood, until now. Please continue to spread awareness so that no one else must suffer from a lack of knowledge! Thank you for educating yourself in knowing what to do to help someone else you may know or care for or for yourself!

INTRODUCTION

I have always known I carry sickle cell otherwise known as having sickle cell trait, ever since my early childhood when I recall often being in such severe pain, bedbound and screaming. The fevers and limb swelling particularly in my forearms and hands was always accompanied with anaemia.

Pain in all my joints and bones of my body especially my legs, arms, ribs and pelvis was so severe, that my poor mother often wouldn't know how best to comfort me. Back then she was just told "it's growing pains!" An often-told misinformation that GPs tend to tell parents with children who carry sickle cell, but now I know it is down to my status in having the trait. Others who I have found with the trait like myself, have confirmed they also have these "growing pains", despite them now being fully grown adults.

This knowledge is now solidified, with me suffering the most debilitating and worst crisis of my life this year in June 2020, the fifteenth to be exact, until September and leaving me with ongoing pains, triggered by vigorous exercise, an issue I've never had before. With little by way of answers from my GP's and no medical help offered to me; I decided that I had enough. So, I began my quest to find answers in the hopes that I would find others like me, who are carriers of sickle cell, but have suffered in silence all their lives and been fobbed off whenever they present in pain or are made to feel as if they are crazy. Another saying I often heard from medics is "it's very rare for carriers to experience symptoms!"

I know it's rare, but yet here I am suffering. I have gone through enough physical pain crisis to know when I am having one. I may never fully understand what I go through, but my belief is that in sharing my personal experiences, it might help shed some light on others' similar experiences.

This is my journey and I hope others who are just as much sickle cell warriors with a symptomatic trait status, as those who are full blown sickle cell anaemia patients find some comfort. Although the trait is not medically classed as a disability, actually in cases like mine, it can leave you feeling and being very disabled with many physical disabilities. As it is a condition which affects the red blood cells and as blood flows everywhere in the body, it therefore affects everything!

"The Lord your God is in your midst, A Warrior who saves. He will rejoice over you with joy; He will be quiet in His love [making no mention of your past sins], He will rejoice over you with shouts of joy".
Zephaniah 3:17 (AMP)

Thank you for seeking answers with me! Let us hope this can change the way carriers are seen and treated in the medical world and therefore save another sickle cell trait warrior's life!

Welcome to my story!

CHAPTER 1A.
WHAT IS SICKLE CELL ANAEMIA?

Sickle Cell Anaemia (Haemoglobin SS) is a genetically inherited red blood cell disorder, which predominantly affects people from Afro-Caribbean ethnic backgrounds and some of Asian heritage, although I have learned this past year (2020) that anyone can have it, including Caucasians from Mediterranean ethnic backgrounds such as from Italy, Spain, Greece and other European countries.

It evolved as a genetic mutation, in countries where Malaria was prevalent. So, it is thought that carriers of Sickle Cell Anaemia, diagnosed as having Sickle Cell Trait, are protected against Malaria due to their carrier status.

Although some publications state that this is not necessarily the case and some have been known to still acquire Malaria

The normal shape of red blood cells is round, but in sickle cell, approximately eighty to one hundred of red blood cells are sickle or 'C' shaped, rigid and stiff, causing them to clump together, blocking blood vessels and causes severe and sometimes crippling episodes of pain. This abnormality in the haemoglobin means that oxygen is not able to be carried through the blood properly to the organs and is known as a vaso-occlusive 'crisis'. This in turn may result in organ damage and can cause severe complications and even death if left untreated.

Crisis pain can last minutes, to hours, to days, weeks and in some instances has been known to last months at a time. Although there are other forms of crisis, this is the most commonly experienced.

The severity and length of this pain varies from individual to individual and can depend on the site of pain on the body and other physiological and environmental factors.

Due to oxygen levels within the red blood cells being depleted, anaemia and chronic fatigue is another presentation individuals with this disorder suffer.

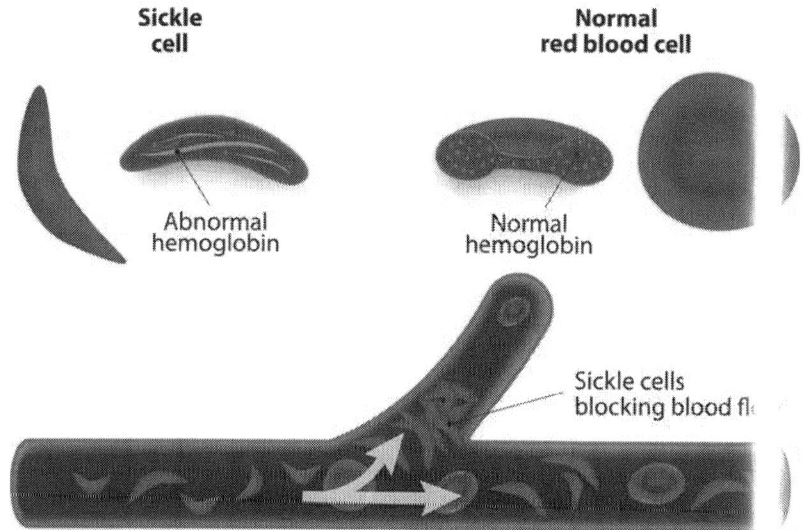

Diagram of Sickled Cells and Normal Red Blood Cells

CHAPTER 1B.
SICKLE CELL TRAIT – A CARRIER'S PERSPECTIVE

Sickle Cell Trait (Haemoglobin AS), otherwise known as Hb AS, is an inherited blood condition, but unlike sickle cell anaemia it is not classified as a disease. It cannot turn into the full-blown disease, but can also cause some problems, as there are a percentage of abnormal red blood cells that a carrier has. As the following diagram depicts, it is genetically inherited from one parent who either is a carrier of the abnormal 'sickled' haemaglobin (S), while the other parent will pass on the gene for normal haemaglobin (A) or if the parent has full blown sickle cell anaemia and passes on the gene for sickled haemaglobin (S).

There is a twenty-five percent chance of the child having sickle cell anaemia, where both parents have sickle cell trait and a twenty-five percent chance of the child inheriting sickle cell trait where one parent has full blown sickle cell anaemia. This percentage increases to fifty percent where one parent has sickle cell anaemia and the other has sickle cell trait. Therefore, it is always worth asking the questions regarding your status when entering into intentional relationships where marriage and children are the intended outcome. Newborn screening tests take place over in the UK as routine screening tests, but if you are unsure, it is always worth requesting a screening test so that you can be sure of your status and can plan ahead accordingly.

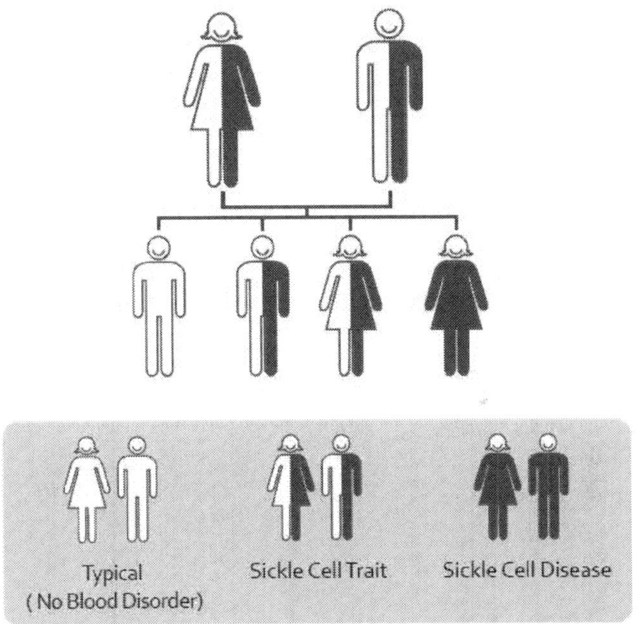

Order of inheritance of Sickle Cell Trait

There are certain circumstances in which carriers can experience crisis, but it is said to be very rare. I will go into what my triggers for crisis are within this book and will provide you with the list of common causes of a sickle cell crisis, just for you to be aware and put in preventative measures for you to protect yourself, regardless of whether you are symptomatic or not. In my experience and since I began meeting many others like me, who are carriers of sickle cell, we have come to know that the misconception of 'carriers present with no symptoms' are not that of our collective experiences.

I have always had symptoms, some of which have been very severe, from the age of five years old!

CHAPTER 2.
JUNE FIFTEENTH 2020 – THE WORST CRISIS I HAVE EVER HAD!

It was a hot summer's day, a day like many others, but because of COVID-19 restrictions, I decided to workout indoors rather than venturing outside to skip for at least twenty minutes. I had just finished working in my newly decorated home office and worked late. I had been feeling extremely fatigued of late and had been planning to take a couple of extra days off from work to just enjoy a long weekend, not to do anything, but just to catch up on some much-needed rest.

I had also been having these really severe headaches since March, which made me extremely nauseous, so I was on medication for those 'Propranolol' and for anti-sickness 'Metoclopramide'. They felt like migraines, but somewhat different, even though they had gotten so bad, I was beginning to become really confused, whilst doing the simplest of things. I did not think much of it as I know my whole family on my mother's side suffer with high blood pressure and my mum herself has been fighting with hypertension (high blood pressure) for at least the past 10 years, with it escalating to hypertensive crisis (critically high) range earlier last year and ongoing at its worst. That was what my GP had suggested that my headaches were also in relation to.

I attended the Accident and Emergency Department (A&E) at my local hospital back in March, when I had ended up off sick from work for three weeks. At the hospital they had a couple of doctors check me out. My eyes had been hurting too since these headaches began and yes, I was very stressed due to how hectic a few things both at home and at work combined were.

One doctor who saw me, felt that I needed a brain scan due to my symptoms to rule out anything sinister, but when I went around to the nurse's station, another doctor that I saw decided that I was okay with slightly elevated blood pressure, but nothing to be worried about and I was told to go back to my community doctor for hypertension medication, regardless of how worried my GP and the one-one-one operator were, which was why I had attended so urgently. Three weeks later, I went back to work, despite the ongoing headaches. I managed the best as I could and then when we began the new ways of working from home, I welcomed it, so that I would be able to try to manage the pounding head pains that I felt and also reduce my stress due to being at home to look after my mum if she needed me.

April and May came and I began wallpapering the house when off work, trying to keep busy and stay productive at weekends. June came and little did I know a loud and very clear warning came about with work carrying out BAME risk assessments for Black and Asian Minority Ethnic staff who appeared to be higher risk of contracting this unknown, scary disease that was affecting the whole world.

When I saw that sickle cell anaemia was on the 'at risk' list, I emailed my line manager to say that I was symptomatic, as a carrier of sickle cell and had suffered with crisis and complications relating to my carrier status, since the age of five and was concerned that I had been attending our community hub base to work on the rota.

I had more than anything been concerned about not self-isolating due to living with my mum, who fell into two of the clinically vulnerable categories as one: she was over seventy years of age and two: she suffered with hypertension, which was dangerously high. Those had been my main concerns and I had also mentioned to a couple of colleagues that I carry sickle cell so needed to be careful, but little did I know that me seeing this risk assessment was a warning of what was to come!

I have often found that when I have ended up really ill such as when I had pneumonia or the time when I suffered with pyelonephritis, my body gets very fatigued and I begin taking specific supplements prior to being diagnosed or going into shock and hospitalized. I have always ended up doing research on the very thing I end up having, literally just before symptoms occurring, as if my body knows it is coming, but my mind does not consciously yet or I crave certain vitamins and mineral supplements.

I now understand that the above subconscious knowledge and feelings of dread that accompany these 'feelings' are actually premonitions, which I realize from reading other warrior's testimonials and these are in actual fact warning signs that foretell bad news for me physically!

So, June fifteenth at approximately six-thirty PM when I had signed off from work, I decided to do a high intensity workout because exercise used to be my thing. The energizing boost I enjoyed which would often pick me up and the afterglow, which made my skin glisten and the rush of endorphins

I felt I so desperately needed to shake off this overwhelming fatigue. I wish I knew just what I was in for!

I began skipping and each time I became breathless I would have to stop and try to breathe, until twelve minutes had passed, and I really began to struggle and wheeze. The windows were wide open, and I had a fan on because I felt I needed some air. "So, I haven't done twenty minutes, but I can't breathe properly, it's okay if I stop!" I reasoned internally to myself. I leaned forward and began gasping for air, inhaling deeply, and exhaling really hard to try to stabilize my breathing. I sat down and felt bad that I could not continue my session, but I felt good that at least I did something!

Later that night, even though the air had cooled down and I had taken a bath, I just felt like I was overheating and just before I got ready for bed, I noticed swelling of my right hand and forearm. I went to show my mum, who stated that my knuckles looked bruised in comparison to my other hand and she reached out to touch my arm, yet even the gentlest brush of her hands against my forearm hurt. It felt almost like the nerves on my skin were on fire and being scratched raw, or that my skin was turned inside out and the raw flesh exposed and being scratched; I cannot describe it any other way. I tried ignoring my arm and going to bed, but by two AM I still couldn't get to sleep, and I ended up with such throbbing pain radiating from my shoulder to my fingers, which looked really swollen and fat.

I was so hot with a fever and shivering so much, that I began sweating and moaning with the pain I was in, so I went to my mum's room and woke her up and let her know I was in agony. Even though I felt exhausted, the pain just wouldn't let me fall asleep. By the time I ended up dozing off it was the latter early hours of the next morning.

I woke up with tenderness in my ribs, a swollen stomach, fever, my arm was immobile by the morning and that was the start of the worst vaso-occlusive pain crisis of my life (this is where the red blood cells clump together blocking blood vessels and prevent oxygen flow to the organs resulting in such crippling pain), with the potential for organ damage, if left untreated, which I was.

CHAPTER 3.
RIDE IT OUT

For the remainder of the following week, I kept calling in to work off sick, due to this swollen right arm causing such throbbing and stabbing pains to radiate the whole length of my arm. I recall being asked what it was and whether or not I had called the doctor. I had explained that I was having a sickle cell pain crisis, and that the doctors don't ever do anything, but I couldn't use my arm!

All the usual symptoms followed, such as fevers, malaise, shooting pains in my arms and legs and in the bony parts of my body. This included having pain in my upper back, spine, pelvis, rib cage, tummy swelling and pains I had never experienced before too, such as stabbing pains in my feet, a stiff neck and such severe stabbing pains in my head. As an already light-skinned black African woman, I ended up looking so pale with no life in my eyes.

This pain would come on so suddenly and I would become so weak, after waking up feeling like I was okay, but upon trying to stand, I would feel as if I was going to collapse and my whole body including my limbs would go limp.

The pain that I was in got so bad, with it especially worsening at nighttime. I ended up feeling so exhausted and so desperate for a good night's sleep, but I forgot what that even felt like during this three-month period of non-stop intermittent agony, which took over my entire body.

Anyone who knows me and my mum, knows I tower over her tiny frame of four feet eleven inches tall, by almost a whole entire foot. I am five feet nine inches tall and over the past couple of years have become quite heavy again in weight, due to immobility issues. I had lost over six stones in body weight prior to my health deterioration, but due to an injury whilst deadlifting eighty-five kilograms in 2015, with no back support in the gym, I ended up with what doctors suspected to be a slipped disc. I realized I should have listened to my instinct and not the personal trainer I was training with, who said I made the lifts look easy.

That kept me down for over a month, right at the start of my business, but I got back up and built my company for the next couple of years. In 2017 I began doing so much, that what I believed at the time to be a slipped disc, my Chiropractor and the A&E consultant I had been seen by, stated it was nothing to do with my spine, it was muscular. I now believe this to be down to my sickle cell trait status, as stress I have recently found out is a major trigger of this type of pain. Although majorly felt within the bones, muscles can be severely affected too. A fact I later came to know.

The pains in my back were so severe, that for months at a time, I could do nothing but sleep. Even waking up to go to the bathroom and relieve myself was hard work and excruciatingly painful. Just lifting my body up from my shoulders and below from my bed required my mum's help. Even lowering myself to use the toilet took me having to lean my back against the wall and sliding down, whilst using one crutch that my brother had given me after he had knee surgery and needed crutches to enable him to move about, following an accidental tear to his knee cap. So, I struggled with no answers for so long, settling into deep depression, whilst wondering what on earth was going on with my body. Little did I know what I would come to discover regarding all those symptoms I described above within the worst year of the nearing future ahead.

From June until September 2020, as these pains riddled every part of my body, I became so afraid of the nighttime, as the temperature would cool down, the sleep just would not come! I do not even know how I made it through this time frame, without stepping into a hospital, as my body was so weak. I knew that death was very close, so I was fighting for my life literally!

With the many times I questioned my very existence and wished for God to take me home. I knew if I had not begun reading up and accessing further advice from the sickle cell society and contacting my local Sickle Cell and Thalassaemia Centre to speak to someone for advice on what to do, I would not have made it, nor would I have been any wiser on how to help myself nor been strong enough to help others who are symptomatic carriers like me.

I found a book written by a parent who carried the trait herself. She also was a carer for her young son, who was diagnosed at birth with full blown sickle cell anaemia (Haemoglobin SS) at its worst form! This book and speaking with a lovely lady, who is a genetics counsellor at my local Sickle Cell and Thalassaemia Service, helped me in ways only God and my mum know, because of the mental and emotional struggle I was battling, alongside such physical torture that my red blood cells were subjecting me to!

I began researching into blood nourishing and haemoglobin building, anti-inflammatory supplements, vitamins and minerals which my body needed in order to replenish, hydrate, alkalise and oxygenate my sickled red blood cells and restore me to full health again.

I knew hydration was vital in order to minimize the pains I felt and also obtained further insight from Tamika Moseley's book, ***"Sickle Cell: Natural Healing, A Mother's Journey!"*** She chronicles her journey as a carrier of sickle cell, who suffered complications whilst in the military and during pregnancies and she advises on how she helped her son with full blown sickle cell anaemia (Hb SS) through natural herbal supplementation and nutrition.

My mum then purchased all the haemoglobin building, nutrient rich, detoxifying, blood cleansing and oxygenating foods and herbs we could access readily online to naturally medicate and treat me. Looking back, I know beyond the shadow of a doubt that I would not be here today, had I not been aware of just what was going on. Four weeks into this crisis, this was mental and physical torture, and I was ready to die!

I am thankful for a praying parent, who stood by me and saw and felt the pain I was going through. She cooked and juiced all the vegetables and pulses we knew to eat and even fed me, because I could not hold cutlery or feed myself for over three months. I needed help to go to the toilet and she bathed me, lifting me in and out of the warm, soothing water to help minimize the pain I was in.

My mum propped me up in bed when I could not even turn or lift myself and the pain, I saw in her eyes, at being so helpless after doing all she could, yet she could not stop me from crying out or screaming. She tirelessly ran to my side at every scream, or whimper. She prayed me through it all and when bewilderment hit with a temporary relief came, she would pray that I had the strength to continue fighting. Mum's prayers gave me the mental resolve to know that good would come out of this traumatic debilitating experience, reminding us both of our humanity and taking me right back to my early childhood into my teens, where at the age of eighteen years old, I had the last severely debilitating crisis, which I thought was bad, but not like this. This was hell, or at least what I thought hell felt like to me!

I recall that every time I ended up bed ridden as a child, the images of me screaming and writhing in such pain, as if my mind was watching a movie set on replay. This was real. This was why so much of my childhood I missed so much school. I was extremely anaemic often in high school, on a monthly basis to be more precise. I missed my mock exams and could not even attend to collect my award at the "Black Achievers Award Ceremony!"

Looking back, I realized I had been conditioned to fight this at a very tender age and I remembered that though these pains and symptoms would come on so suddenly, they just as quickly would go! All I knew and remembered was that as a child and in the last major pain crisis in my teenage years, I was really sick for over eight weeks and then it went and life would return to normal, whatever that was!

Yet here I was at thirty-five years old and no doctor had taken notice of me. Not one had taken me seriously and when I had called up to ask for blood tests I was informed "You'll have to wait for things to return to normal, whenever that will be due to COVID-19!" I could have died for all that doctor was even bothered and this affected me mentally and emotionally and continued my total lack of trust in the medical world to help me and others who suffered just like I was and continue to do!

That call to my doctor asking for my blood count to be taken, was made in June 2020, but it was ignored and yet here again as I was used to since my early childhood, I had to just ride it out. I gave all I had and held onto the faith inside of my heart and soul, even when I wanted to let go, that faith and my mum's prayers just would not let me give up!

4TH July 2020 - During my crisis, in so much pain, with a low grade fever, exhausted and confused

22nd September 2020 - In crisis and unable to sleep due to pain

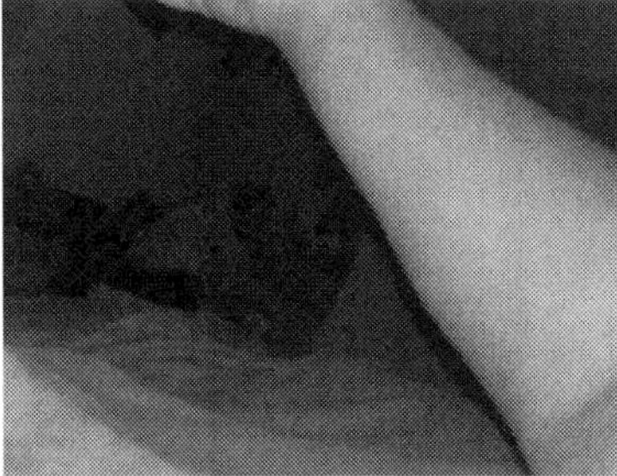

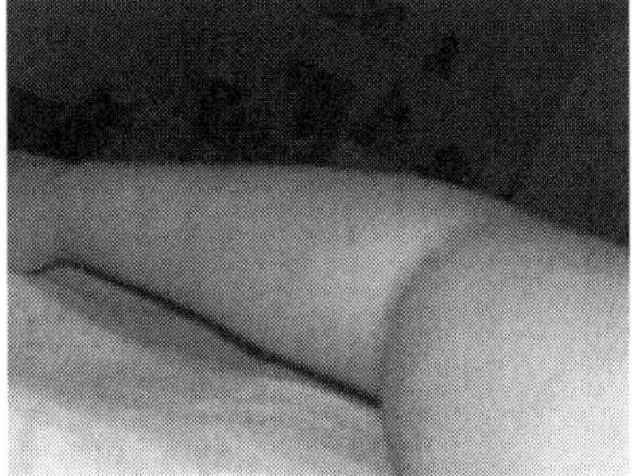

23rd July 2020 Swelling of my right arm

Facial swelling 4th Aug 2020

Laying down in the sun under my window trying to absorb the heat in my bones.

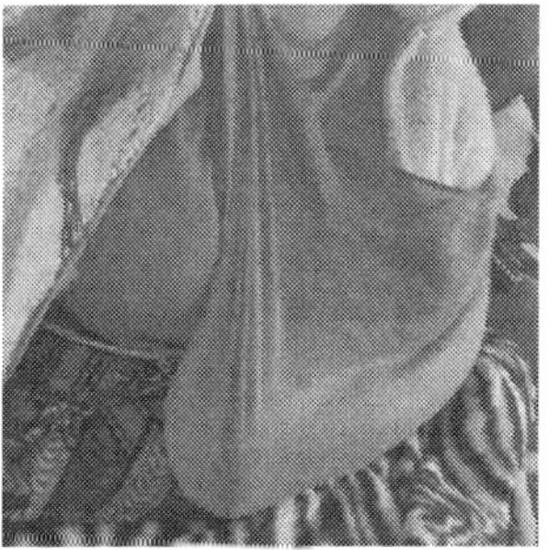

29th August 2020 - In so much pain, I could not use my arm and my mum made a makeshift sling to support my my arm.

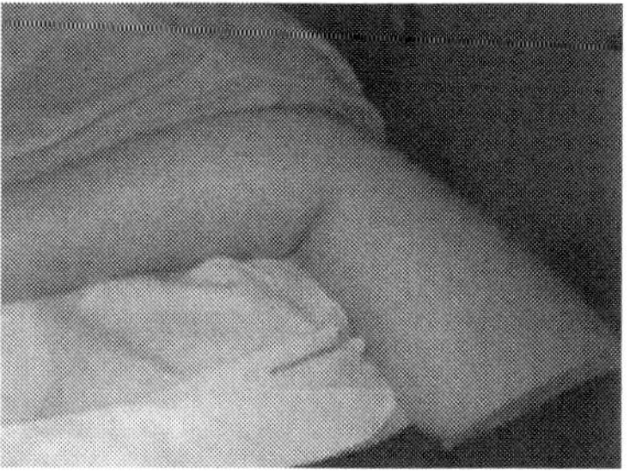

22nd September 2020 – my arm was on fire and I was in crisis

CHAPTER 4.
MEMORIES AND FLASHBACKS

Following the last ten month's painfully debilitating experiences, I can recall several occasions in my twenties, where I experienced similar pains as the ones which I previously described. There are far too many to recount them all, but some certainly stand out more than others, which had me screaming out or crying in agony or both!

A particular time I recall running home one Christmas Eve in 2012. I was travelling and working as a locum Band four Associate Practitioner within Histopathology and Immunohistochemistry to and from Sheffield in South Yorkshire, which took me three hours each way, from where I was living in Horsforth, Leeds. I used to be a keen runner, who the majority of the time was pain free whilst running, with occasional struggles in breathing or unexplainable sharp pains and muscle cramps. Up until then, I managed myself and my health as well as I could.

As it was winter and a very cold and snow filled one at that, I was really hoping that I got back to Leeds by train early enough to catch the last bus home. Bearing in mind, all public transport this side of the country stops running early on Christmas Eve and buses headed to Horsforth were not great at any time of the year, let alone during bad weather or bank holidays.

I realized I had missed the last bus homeward bound though, when I got to Leeds around seven PM and much of the city centre was empty. My long run home began in the cold snow. I got as far as Kirkstall Road where the Health Centre is – so approximately one and a half miles to two miles out of the city centre, then I felt this excruciating pain stabbing right through my right hip and I had no choice, but to stop running and begin walking, if you could call hobbling slowly walking.

I felt cold to the bone as the snow had drenched me through by this time, despite my layers and thin wind breaker. I did try to stop and bend down to rummage in my big running backpack to find my purse, but it was so much effort in the steady, but heavy snowfall, with frozen fingers. So, I continued limping on, almost in tears.

What should have taken me under an hour running, took me approximately two and a half hours, in the freezing cold and with such a painful limp. I got home and ran upstairs to go and shower, not thinking much of it through.

Later that night after I had warmed up and was cozy in bed, I ended up in such pain that I could not stay laid down. I got up and rang my mum, who was retired, but volunteering at a Bible College in the Netherlands. She was my go-to whenever I felt ill or sick or upset, my best friend. Despite our differences of opinion on many aspects of my life, and from the typical older generation, we had the usual strict African parent-child relationship growing up. We had grown very close through specific traumatic points in my life and I knew she would pick up my call no matter how late it was.

I rang her crying hysterically down the line, that she had a hard time hearing what I was saying. Eventually, I muttered out the words "I'm in so much pain, I can't sleep!" Going on to explain and describe the pain I was in, we both realized that these were the all too familiar stabbing pains I had often felt in my childhood, teenage years and beyond, so I cried and sobbed until my poor mum was so tired, she began to fall asleep whilst still on the phone to me. I cannot recall how I eventually fell asleep, but I did. When I woke up the next morning, I decided a long hot shower would help me to function, because my hands were in so much pain, I could hardly use them to do anything for myself and I felt absolutely chilled to the bone.

It was early Christmas morning 2012 and it was my first Christmas back in Leeds and the first spent living with my boyfriend at the time, so as ill as I felt, I was super excited and I wanted it to be perfect. Boy had I got a surprise in store for him of what I was going to cook. I had it all planned out! This was going to be a feast which would not easily be forgotten! However, I did not realize just how much of a challenge I had in store. I had no idea just how I was going to cook whilst my hands were so sore, they had swollen overnight and my joints hurt with every utensil I tried to hold.

I had woken up with what I felt was a bad case of flu. I was too late to pick up a turkey or lamb leg in the local supermarket earlier the weekend before, they had all sold out, but I ended up buying the biggest whole chicken I could find. I had seasoned my chicken the night before, but I had not as yet cut the string off which was holding the stuffing inside. I screamed out, as quietly as I could, as I did not want my boyfriend to know how much of a struggle simple tasks were proving to be, but then I called for him to come help me hold the knife and cut the string off. He did and I bolted from the room as quickly as I could and shot up the stairs to the first-floor bathroom where I violently vomited into the toilet.

When I got back downstairs, the look of dismay on his face as he questioned what's wrong and why I threw up! I guess he thought I might have been pregnant, yet again, as we had previously gone through the whole trauma of an unplanned pregnancy and I delivered prematurely at six months' gestational age, where complications and infection almost caused me to lose my life. I will go into a little more detail with regards to this later on in my re-collections.

As I was always good at pretending where my emotions were concerned, I told him as convincingly as I could that I just did not feel very well, but I was okay and prompted him to go and sit back down and relax in the living room, so I could surprise him! He did and I continued, in pain, as best as I could. It took me longer than usual, but I muddled through and focused on the outcome I so wanted. He always enjoyed my cooking, so I did my best and when I was finished, the table was full of all sorts of delicacies and different dishes, thankfully with enough left over for the coming few days that followed, so I could rest, as I ended up having to take some time off work due to how ill I was.

Christmas Eve 2012 – drenched, frozen
I made it home, despite the hip pain.
I was still smiling as it was my first
Christmas back in Leeds

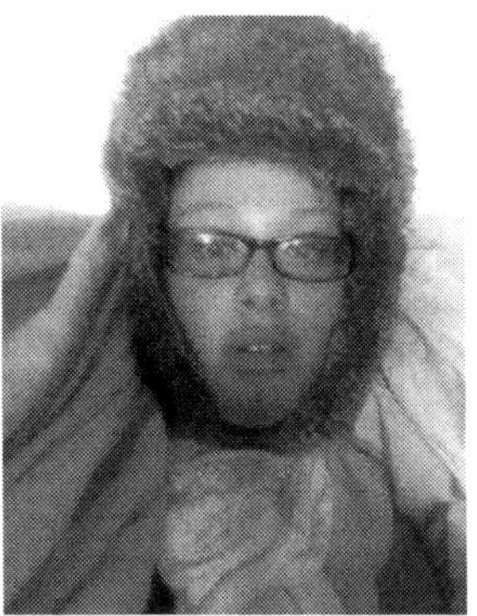

27th December 2012, but
unable to go to work
and laying down well
wrapped up on the sofa
with flu and in crisis

Looking back in hindsight, now I specifically remember that I had a few of these pain crisis episodes throughout the year, from October 2012 until I moved house again in November 2013, with frequent ill health due to chest infections, which seemed to take absolutely ages to go.

I recall my boss in the Histopathology Lab in which I was locumming in Sheffield at the time stating that "it was not normal for a healthy twenty-eight-year-old woman to be unable to cope with lack of sleep and travelling six hours to and from work daily, it must be that I need to sort out my domestic issues!" If only she had known just what I was up against, she would have known better. Had I realized what I now fully am aware of, I would have defended myself in that specific conversation a little more and most likely been accessing the right help before now. Although it was absolutely none of her business, I was just too exhausted both from my physical pain and also from some unrelated difficulties on the home front to be the usual feisty, stand-up for myself version of myself.

Being a Senior Biomedical Scientist and my boss, I fully feel that it was wrong for her and anyone else within the work force I have worked under since her, who may have stated these "ignorant, passive-aggressive, snide" remarks. I had multiple experiences of pain crisis and of comments about my 'poor health' as a student living in Manchester from 2009 until moving back to Leeds in 2012. Though my crisis episodes lasted just a couple of weeks at a time when I was in my mid to late twenties or periods of chronic fatigue and also recall suffering with severe problems with my periods, which I now know are linked, I just got on with them, but knowing what I do now, I would have fought just that little bit harder to be seen and heard by medics. At one point I recall stating to a friend that "I may as well work until I collapse, before going back to the doctor!" I wish they knew how they make people feel, the ones we are supposed to trust in restoring our health actually becoming an enemy, or what so often felt like one!

I was made to feel like there was no point in seeking their help! I could name and shame a few, but it would not make all these past misfortunes go away. Instead, I record my tale in here for you, the reader to help yourself and know that if this is ongoing with you, you MUST seek help and show them my book. I recommend anyone with any medical undiagnosed concern to take heart and keep pushing too. This although specifically catered to sickle cell trait and the mysteries of why some of us carriers experience the symptoms in the ways that we do and as I have, this same persistence will not go amiss if you keep pestering your doctors, they will have to refer you on for the relevant testing after numerous requests.

I guarantee it will not be the last symptomatic sickle cell trait presentation in the world that is written as a story book out there, the more voices that rise up and speak out against this inequality of number one; recognition because of not having a definitive diagnosis of a recognized condition and number two, because it is not physically always visible to the naked eye; the better recognized it will become!

Sickle Cell Anaemia comes under the Equality Act 2010, but it does not include Sickle Cell Trait. However, I write to hopefully make a change in that too so that when we experience any ill health in relation to our status as carriers, we are not penalized for it, as it is completely out of our control, yet it can be extremely debilitating and without the appropriate help in diagnosis and recognition, people will die! I would have died had it not been for my elderly and very unwell mother looking after me whilst she was in a state of hypertensive crisis. However, she never goes to medical doctors for help, because she knows how they have always made her feel and that says a lot. The fact that someone would rather die in a so called "civilized, first class world" country or as my Grandpa would say "bwana land" meaning the "white man's country" than to access their very top-notch medical care says a lot! If it had not been for mummy's faith upholding the both of us and her stance to stand firm on the Word of God, we both would not have made it to this day! All I know is, we prayed and asked for direction and guidance on which herbal supplements to take during the worst and continued management of my crisis and of what to buy to help manage my pain and my mother's ill health too and later bought as much as we could. Though really traumatic, this whole painful spell has drawn my heart back to the Lord. I learned to trust in Him and again reconcile to and choose to live for Him. The meaning of walking by faith became so very real to me. Led by faith, we surely were!

Another very recent episode of pain occurred almost as soon as I began my new job in 2018. I would walk the two-point three-mile journey home and detour to my niece's child minder to collect her adding an additional half a mile to my journey each way. All of a sudden, I began experiencing sharp, stabbing pains in my right hip, which I can only describe as a sensation of my hip joints rubbing and scraping against each other. I even began thinking my bones were rotting away, because I could not walk, or weight bare for months. Just as suddenly as it came on, this pain just disappeared. I cannot even recall the exact moment it went away, but it did result in me suffering a prolonged, excruciating case of plantar fasciitis.

This pain went on for approximately nine months non-stop. I remember waking up in the middle of the night and being unable to stand, let alone walk to go to the bathroom. My mum came to my rescue. She would get iced bottles of water and put them under my feet to help reduce the swelling. I ended up having to purchase a bike on the cycle to work scheme, just to reduce the pressure and pain on my feet, which did greatly help me and made it easier picking up my niece from school.

The day my bike got delivered to work and I collected my niece from her child minders. 30th April 2018

I feel now that this was related, as my feet have swollen a lot over this past year, although the pains within them are in the same place as I experienced this plantar fasciitis previously. It was not prolonged though this time and the crisis in my feet would be present only for a few moments each time, albeit frequently.

Yet another time I experienced such excruciating pain are at times where I have had the flu. Now to most, physicians say it is very rare to have the flu, but I reckon I get at least one bad case of flu every other year. Or it might just be that I have a cold and then my body ends up so weak immune health wise, that the accompanying stabbing pains which cause me to have to crawl to the toilet because I physically have become so weak to get out of bed, that I had easily mistaken these episodes for the flu. Even lifting the covers off myself has always hurt my arms and hands so much, that I have fought to just force myself to fall off my bed when I am this sick. Eating does not appeal to me when I have been in this physical condition, because I literally have no energy to do so, but I do hydrate very well when I am in this state. I know when I become very stressed, that I tend to become very sick. I know when I was fired from my job, in 2017 for asking for a reference for a full-time role, due to my deteriorating health, the heightened stress levels caused me to become really unwell as above. That particular episode of pain was concentrated especially within my swollen stomach, limbs and tender ribs and stabbing pains within my chest and lasted about four weeks then, with needing additional rest time after getting in from work on an evening, to fully recover. My close friend and sister, I call her 'baji' was supposed to be visiting and I had to postpone our visit due to not wanting to make her unwell and because I could not get out of my bed for this period of time and it just would not have been any fun!

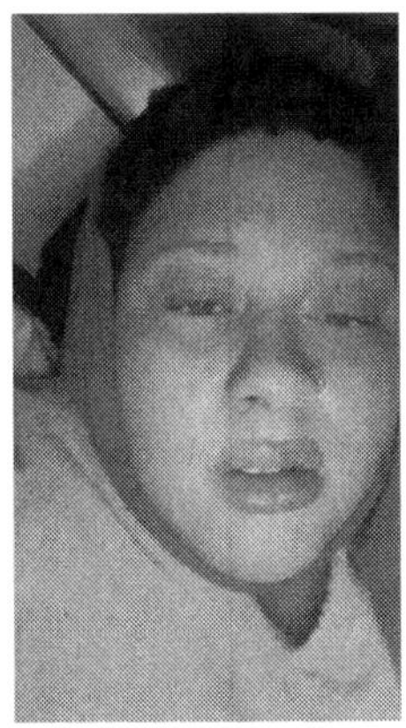

Left to right - 13th & 14th February 2018 – really unwell with the flu and such pain in all my joints. I literally was crying lifting my covers from my skin, when the pain was at it's worst.

I have observed that on a few occasions over the past couple of years more than ever, my stomach had swollen up and it hurt to the touch. Once I thought I had a bout of gastroenteritis, as my stomach had also been quite upset, accompanied with nausea. This often happened when I had experienced pain crisis. Because it has occurred at random times, I never thought it was linked to my crisis, until this most recent severe one.

As it would go and come back every so often throughout this latest prolonged period, I now know it is all related and my body just went through hell with all my systems wreaking havoc, because of my poorly oxygenated blood flow. I ended up having my stool tested and it came back as normal this time, but it was very different to what is normal for me. I will not go into a full description, but just so you are aware of what to look out for, I will briefly explain.

Usually, I did not suffer with constipation, due to a high dietary fibre intake, this is not quite the opposite either, but it did always feel easy to pass. However, at some stage through my tummy swelling, my stool had become a mustard yellow in colour and extremely 'mushy' looking. I had researched into sickle cell anaemia enough to know that this can be an indication of liver complications, so if ever you feel like this is abnormal for you, please go and get it checked out pronto.

Thankfully, I had nothing to worry about these past couple of times. I feel like my stomach looked pregnant with the pain being increasingly unbearable and really hot to the touch during this episode, but then again within a few hours or days or weeks it went away as suddenly as it came on. This has always been typical with swelling of my limbs too though, so it was never isolated to just my stomach, although the swelling can disappear with my stomach and still be present with my arms or feet.

I've often been told my body is weak, as it seemed I was always getting sick. I remember my cousin once mentioned that in passing and it always stood out in my mind, that this actually rang true.

As afore mentioned, in my teenage years and often at high school, I would often miss a lot of precious school time. One particular school trip stuck out to me and the years of excruciating events which followed it with regards to my periods, which I now know were extremely painful and heavy due to my sickle cell trait status. Something I did not realize whilst growing up. It was a regular school day, in my Chemistry lesson and I was chosen to take part in an extracurricular class. I was on a school visit attending another school and sat with my girlfriends, in a group on a table in the middle of the classroom and I began rocking backwards and forwards moaning.

My friends had to signal to our Teacher at the front of the class to come and get me, because I was literally trembling by this time and my pain level was fast rising. Bless my Teacher, I was a slender build, yet athletic with the typical African features of wide hips and large buttock region and the smallest waist and broad shoulders, who towered over my very petite, Geordie, chemistry Teacher.

My Teacher took one look at my face and knew something was off. She came and got me from where I was sat and took me on the long winding path to the School Nurses office. I recall her telling me that I looked 'green', and I was trembling so violently, she thought I was going to faint whilst we were walking.

I felt so nauseous, feverish and lightheaded with severe stabbing pubic bone pains and period cramps too. Anyway, we finally got to the Nurses office and I remember feeling an urgent need to relieve myself, as I often do at the onset of my monthly cycle and I got stuck feeling so unwell in the toilet, I had no energy to get up.

This, of course worried both my Teacher and the School Nurse, but eventually I managed to freshen myself up after what must have been 20 minutes just sitting there trying to obtain the energy to use the bathroom and function on my own. The Nurse then administered some pain-relieving medication, gave me some cool water to drink and gave me a hot water bottle and I was allowed to fall asleep for the duration of the afternoon in the little single bed that was in there.

I have never, ever been to another Nurses Station in a school ever since, but I recall relaying the story to my mum and never forgetting that rather embarrassing school trip, yet I had never been so grateful for such a great Nurses station within a school either.

The trip was supposed to have been a treat as part of the Gifted and Talented Project, which included extra support and additional field trips for students who seemed to excel with their studies.

I also recall missing my mock GCSE exams due to being severely anaemic for over 8 weeks, that all I remember doing was sleeping. My mum recalls having to wake me up just to get me to eat, which was such an effort and off back to sleep I would go.

This began a long list of missed events to this day!

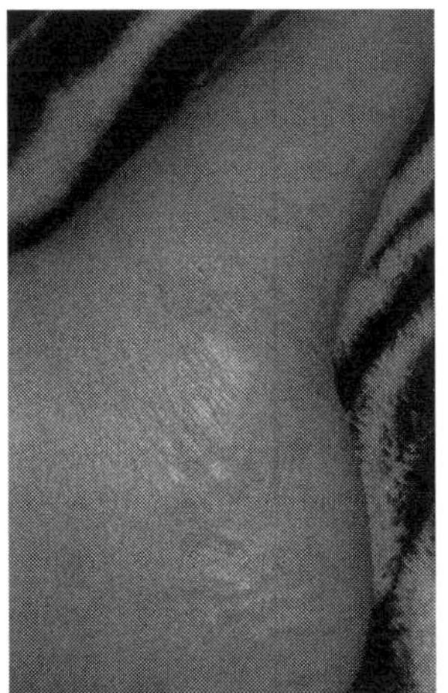

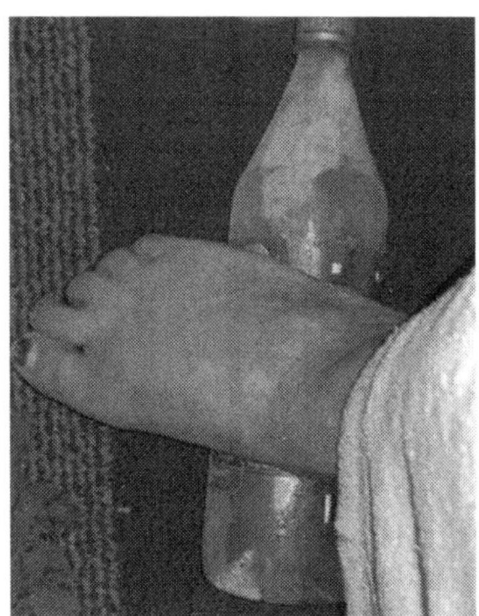

Left to right images - 29th March 2018 and 3rd April 2018 - getting in from work and having to roll my feet on iced bottles of water to reduce the inflammation and pain from plantar fasciitis, which lingered for over nine months of the year and then suddenly disappeared just as suddenly it came on.

CHAPTER 5.
SERIOUS COMPLICATIONS:

MY FIRST PREGNANCY – MISSED MISCARRIAGE - ? PLACENTAL ABRUPTIO

What I have realized over the years is that my body cannot seem to carry children. I now know for certain why, following some similarities which occurred within this last year. So now, I must share. Plus, I have researched into sickle cell pregnancy complications and it appears that they are commonly experienced within the wider sickle cell community. Although not everybody with the trait or full-blown sickle cell disease experiences premature births or such life-threatening complications, mine were very traumatic and the second time proved almost fatal for me too.

The outcome of both pregnancies is that I lost both my children, sadly because of gross medical negligence and due to not being listened to when I said something was very wrong! I had grown accustomed to being made to feel that it was all in my head, until something very bad happened, but by then it was too late because I was in hospital or very sick, but hey, 'doctors are experts,' especially of rare none well researched illnesses, (said sarcastically)!

With the first pregnancy, I felt quite early on, that my baby was sitting very low in my pelvis. I kept having these stabbing pains in my pubic bone throughout and could not eat anything without violently vomiting through my nose, up until just days prior to delivering. My poor mother was so afraid that I would end up being fed intravenously.

It was the morning of April thirtieth, 2002 and I remember going to the Job Centre to sign on for income support, as I was too unwell to work.

It is a kind of blur how the days just before passed, but I physically felt something was wrong. I recall asking the job centre whether I could use their customer toilet, as I was desperate to relieve myself by the time I arrived there. I was just one day short of being six months' pregnant, which I told them of. I ended up with sharp stabbing pains in my lower abdomen and was not allowed to use their bathroom. The reason I was given was that they disallowed the public to use their toilets, due to drug misuse in the past being a problem. I went on to become quite upset and angry because of the increasing pain I was in. I informed them of something I had been told, that if a pregnant lady needs to relieve herself and there is a Policeman/woman nearby, they are obligated to allow the pregnant lady to utilize their hat to relieve herself and they are to shield her. I did later look that up and found it to be true in the law. They just looked at me and told me to go to find another place to go. The awkward location of where they were situated within the city centre made this an awfully difficult task.

I remember hardly being able to walk due to the increase in this sharp pain. I felt I would end up having an accident whilst still in the street. My mother and I continued walking, searching for somewhere close that I could go to relieve myself of a full bladder and stop this pain. I do recall vaguely finding somewhere and being close to tears by the time we got there, but it was such a painful experience that I cannot recall the details fully.

Later that night, I ate something at approximately nine PM and then fell asleep. Around midnight on the first of May, I woke up with excruciating pains, which I knew were contractions, although I was still having a hard time believing I was actually pregnant due to not showing. I was quite slim still, my stomach did not protrude and I felt no movement, except for the pain and constant vomiting and being unable to eat properly, until that particular night.

We called for a family friend to collect my brother, who was happy he could have a mid-week sleepover, so that my mother could accompany me to the hospital and we were driven there. When I got to the maternity ward, I was not checked or examined or given an ultrasound. In actual fact, I was turned away as the scanning machine was broken and just told that it was most likely a 'urine infection' and the 'Braxton Hicks' also known as the pre-contractions, which tend to occur in preparation for active labour from around six months onwards. We got home and I cannot remember what else happened, but it was around two-thirty AM by then, so I ate a bite and went to sleep.

The very next day I recall being brought toweling nappies as a gift by a close family friend, whom I called my Aunty as part of my new "mum-to-be" gifts. We were all sitting on the sofa of our living room and all of a sudden, my belly came alive and I saw what I can only describe as punching and kicking movements frantically coming from within my stomach, as if my little one was screaming "Get me out of here!" I was shocked, as up until that moment, I could not tell that I was pregnant and had never felt any movement.

Anyways, I made it through the day of the first of May following that surprise kicking episode that my baby decided to spring on me. I remember looking at my mum and I told her "We need to get ready; he is coming soon!" Little did I know just how soon. That night just before I went to bed, I had something to eat at approximately nine PM again. The next thing I recall is waking up at midnight and burying my head in a pillow. Sounds that resembled a little something like a roaring lion were coming from my throat. I was so sure the whole street could hear me! My mum then called for an ambulance and I was taken to the hospital where later that night my baby arrived. When we initially arrived, the same midwife who saw me and sent me home the night before, was on shift and as I was not fully dilated, they did not rush to prepare things in anticipation of my baby boy's arrival. I recall being extremely tired and wanted to try going natural, but ended up having such painful contractions that I took gas and air. A little while later, after I gave everyone a shock because the active labour, they did not think I was in, began and my baby boy was coming. So, in a mad panic, the paediatrician and a team of student doctors arrived after being paged by the worried midwives and Mandy, the midwife with blonde hair in a bob was in there assisting.

My little one was born breach later that night into the early hours of the morning. Despite the paediatrician's efforts to turn him around and his strong little heartbeat being heard during this time, all I recall was being told he was still-born and the midwife, Mandy, who turned me away the night before, had blood shot eyes and she did not need to mouth the words, "I'm sorry", I felt she was saying with the look in her tear-filled eyes!

I know that all being as they should have been, my little boy would have lived. If only they had listened to me. Later that week, when I was discharged home, the stabbing pubic bone pains began again and would suddenly just occur as I was standing or walking and then disappear just as quickly as they began.

"68 But He chose the tribe of Judah (as Israel's leader), Mount Zion, which He loved (to replace Shiloh as His capital).

69 And He built His sanctuary (exalted) like the heights (of the heavens), Like the earth which He has established forever."

Psalm 78:68-69 (AMP)

CHAPTER 6.
EXTREME TEMPERATURE CHANGES – HOT TO COLD

Just before my eighteenth birthday, I was enroute to Hawaii for my cousin's wedding. I felt after the previous year's trying events, I so needed this break and to see my family again.

I had not seen my Aunty, my mum's younger sister for over fifteen years, when my brother and I were children in Zambia. I was fine travelling with no sleep on the first part of my journey at night by coach to London Heathrow Airport.

The first flight to San Francisco where I was in transit for five hours went smoothly and then I got to Hawaii another five hours later. Without going into this part of my story in detail, after sleeping for what seemed a very short time after being reunited with my family and talking late into the early hours. I ended up having the worst cramp in my leg that night.

During my stay, fatigue hit me quite bad and to be honest, I was having a hard time keeping up with the rest of my cousins, Aunties' and Uncles staying up so late every night, catching up, though I truly did enjoy every moment of it at the time.

When I finally travelled back home a week later, I ended up having another really severe crisis and was extremely anaemic for over eight weeks. I guess the cause was a combination of things including fatigue, with lack of sleep, the extreme change in temperature coming from a really hot and humid climate back to where it was winter woolly wearing time here.

Whatever caused it, it was bad!!! I even ended up having to leave my new job, because I could not handle being fired, so I left before they had the opportunity to fire me! Again, this is another cycle which continued all throughout my working life.

CHAPTER 7.
PNEUMONIA – ACUTE CHEST SYNDROME

In 2006, I remember feeling extremely ill and kept experiencing such bad chest pains and fevers, which would suddenly go and then come back. I kept going to my doctors to obtain a diagnosis and the right medication, but kept being told that it was a viral chest infection and it would go on its own. This continued for three months from the middle of March to mid-June. I had been booked to go on holiday abroad with my friends, to Spain and the week before we travelled, I was afraid I would not make it, because of this excruciating pain I was in where it felt as if I could not breathe and everything felt like I was being squeezed tightly.

I woke up feeling fine on the day we were flying, so I decided to go away and it seemed for that week that the blazing sunshine and sea breeze did me the world of good, until I got back home. When I returned back to the UK, again the chest pains returned and I felt really ill. I went to the GP, who could see from my records that I had been presenting with the same ongoing problems for some time. I returned home and was told to just ride it out and it should go in a few weeks. That same night, my teeth began chattering and I was frozen to the bone. This was really unusual considering it was the hottest summer the UK had seen for a while. My mum heard me crying in my room and she brought me a cup of hot peppermint tea. I was actually wearing fluffy pajamas and already had a thick winter duvet covering me, but no matter what I just could not get warmed up.

My mum ended up sleeping in my bed, to ensure that she was with me in case my condition worsened overnight. The next morning, she helped get me bathed and dressed and took me to the hospital. When we got there, we were sat in the A&E waiting room and my mum went to ask the receptionist whether I could have a blanket, she was directed to the nurse's station. She went to ask for a blanket and informed the staff that I was really cold. This then prompted them to see me rather quickly and I was told that my oxygen levels were so low, I could have gone into a coma. I was admitted straight away. I had been told that my chest needed an x-ray to see whether I had any fluid in my lungs, but the doctors did not see anything and then I was placed within a general ward, where I kept getting worse. This continued until I recall being on my monthly cycle, a few days later and ended up being rescued from the toilet room next to my bed, as I just had no energy to lift myself up.

The doctors decided to do a chest x-ray, from my bed, which I cannot remember happening. I had been diagnosed with pneumonia and spent the rest of my in-patient visit on the clinical high dependency unit hooked up to oxygen and drifting in and out of consciousness for the duration of my hospital stay. My friend's mum was the sister there in charge of my care at the time and she took such good care of me, including giving me a bed bath, to which I was extremely grateful for. I felt death was so near and I spent the next week physically weak, struggling to breathe and fighting for my life.

That was another scary and very close call! Although I did end up recovering, my chest has never been the same again. I still struggle to breathe since having pneumonia, even though my spirometer tests come back fine every time, I fight for each deep breath I so often need to take. If only I was prescribed medication or flagged as high risk and had my symptoms investigated properly before being admitted into hospital, I wonder whether I would have ended up so unwell, but I guess I will never know now.

This photo was taken just days before I ended up hospitalised with pneumonia in July 2006 and I was severely unwell, yet I don't look sick. I felt fine whilst out in the sun, but ended up severely ill immediately upon my return the following week, just like I had been the three months before going away.

CHAPTER 8.
PREGNANCY NUMBER TWO – UNPLANNED, BUT SO WANTED

Although unplanned by either myself or my boyfriend at the time, I ended up pregnant for the second time in 2007 and was losing blood at just nine weeks when I found out. Petrified and already not in my mum's good books, I was so afraid to tell her that I had gotten myself into this predicament. Firstly, my boyfriend did not want any more children, he already had two.

So, there I was pregnant and alone.

At nine weeks gestational age, I began a heavy bleed. I was temping for work and working two jobs. One of which was immediately as soon as I had finished my day job, so I used to run the ten minutes away to ensure I had enough time to earn a good weekly, extra income. I realize now how much I was hurting my body. I remember getting home, not being able to eat and falling on my huge sofa in fits of tears, crying because my body felt so worn and weak. The exhaustion I felt daily after a full day of work, I did not know just what my body was about to face, all I knew was no amount of sleep would help me. I ended up taking off a week here and there of a job which was not permanent, the agency were not happy at all, but I literally would tremble from fatigue, so it could not be helped. My mum's friend would call me to just shower me with love on the evenings and she was a gift of love to my heart, though grieving through her own very recent loss of her husband.

My doctor demanded me to be on bed rest, telling me that my partner or my mum NEED to come and look after me or I would miscarry. My worst fears surfacing, I could not lose my baby again! The choice was simple, if my boyfriend did not want my child, then he could not have me! So, I did not tell him how sick I was and just managed at home on my own. My mum would call daily to check on me, but our relationship at that point was so strained, I could not tell her of what the doctor had said.

Later, when my mum found out just how sick I had become during this early stage of pregnancy, she came and brought me her delicious homemade chicken and vegetable soup with dumplings. It was the middle of winter; my birthday had passed and she saw how ill I was. It was decided that I would go and live with my mum until my baby was born and then I would find a job after he was six months old. After all, I had gotten myself into this, I now needed to figure out how I would look after myself, my child and my mum, if I was going to be living with her again. I would never ask a man for money, let alone a man I was not married to, so I chose that I would not even bother with asking for child support. I would do it myself!

After moving back in with my mum, I was in so much pain again in the lower pelvis area. It felt like my bladder was always full. I could hardly walk a few seconds and I would get an overwhelming urge to 'wee'. The agency ended up firing me, because yet again, it was January 2008 and I had been off work sick, twice now since that first time I was on bed rest.

Mum and I had a lot of emotional baggage to work through, which we had plenty of time to do, whilst I was there. However, the concern I saw in her eyes as she began getting excited to be a grandmother to her first living grandchild, although seeing her daughter so sick was beginning to really worry her. I could not move much without being in such pain or doubling over grabbing my crotch area, which when I was out in public proved to be rather embarrassing!

One morning a week prior to Valentine's Day, February ninth, 2008, I woke up and my mum and my Aunty were engaged in prayer over the telephone as they did on a daily basis for as long as I can remember. This morning in particular, I am so grateful for those prayers, as I believe they kept both me and my child alive and well for as long as we were!

I went to the toilet as I usually did first thing on a morning after waking up. As I thought it might be nice to go back to bed, I kept the lights off, it was around eight-thirty AM. As I cleaned myself and got up to get dressed, something felt very wrong. My clothes felt wet, this could not be good, as my baby had not as yet reached five months gestationally.

All of a sudden, panic set in and I turned the bathroom light on and screamed "*NO!*" I had begun bleeding extremely heavily. It was gushing out from me, different to the bleed I had earlier in the pregnancy, yet similar, because I knew that this was a sign of miscarriage. I put a sanitary towel on and went to lay back down in my mum's bed so that I could be comforted with the first thing we always used to do and still do to this day in a state of crisis or emergency or following a serious incident, prayer. I know for sure that prayer changes things! Regardless of what it looks like.

Mum and my big Aunty prayed and declared God's will be done in my life and cried out aloud for the Lord to keep both myself and my precious little miracle alive.

I bathed as quickly as I could at home, whilst my mum grabbed me some essentials from my bedroom and sanitary products. I felt that I could not leave the house without first cleaning myself up, as I didn't know whether I would be delivering that very day or not and my personal hygiene was of utmost importance if so! I had never before left my house without bathing, so I was not going to start now!

We then called an ambulance and I was taken into the maternity ward, them thinking I was in active labour, but this appeared to not be the case. However, my cervix was dilated, although not fully and I was bleeding, so heavily, I flooded the toilet the first night I stayed on the ward. Thankfully, my mum was allowed to stay with me. Afraid and undergoing one of the scariest experiences I have ever had to go through. I paled in complexion, losing pints of blood combined with large clots, this should not be happening. I got the sudden urge to 'push' whenever I did go to the bathroom.

The midwife looking after me that night was amazing! I was informed about the fact that I was not dilated enough, but I was opening up slowly and my baby's amniotic sac was still intact, meaning that I needed bed rest and that he would come when he was ready. I was told, in an almost dissuasive way, that I could have a stitch put into my cervix, to ensure he stayed inside of me, but would need to remain on bedrest to prevent premature labour. The pressure I felt under to not have a stitch put in to seal my gradually opening cervix, as I kept being told "*we may rupture the sac and cause him to be born earlier than if nature runs its course*!" The fear that phrase filled both me and my mum with. So, I opted for all things natural and to just let nature take its course. I do recall being given a pessary though.

Looking back, that pessary was to speed up the process. So, night number one and I spent it fervently crying and pleading with the Lord to save my little one's life. I did not care what happened to mine at that point. Not one of my friends nor family was informed of the seriousness of the situation, until a sister friend of my mum's; also a fervent prayerful, faith-filled woman of God, I called her Aunty Carole, called when I was later moved to the pre-natal unit and after speaking with mum asked to come and visit us, as she had felt something was wrong, even though it was not verbalized aloud. Both myself, mum and Aunty Carole knew that when you are praying and believing for a miracle, it is not wise to let many know what you are believing for so that doubt does not creep in and we needed to keep standing in faith until whatever the end outcome was to be, so all everyone was told is, "All is well!" I kept reading the Biblical story of the ***Shunamite woman in 1 Kings 17:17-24*** over and over again and believing that my little one would make it home safely in my arms. With my whole heart, I believed this and kept visualizing my baby and I at home cuddled up safe and warm.

I had a bad first night, that by the next morning the toilet bowl was filled to the brim and overflowed. Not going into details, but when I kept informing the medical staff who were on duty of the toilet not flushing, because of my bleeding and also needing to open my bowels several times that night due to taking the pessary earlier, human waste in all its vile glory filled my bathroom floor and leaked out into the room I was in. I could not believe how slack the level of care was! It was the cleaner who we complained to and she finally got the ward staff to move me into a different room as quickly as possible, so she could disinfect and clean mine for someone new to move into.

After three days spent on the maternity ward, I was sent to a pre-natal unit, where other expectant mothers who either were not quite ready to deliver were kept. I was visited by a Consultant Pediatrician, who kept politely informing me of how high my infection markers were and of her advice, which was to terminate my pregnancy. How could I even think or consider doing that to my own baby? I could feel every movement, every kick, every flutter he brought me such joy! Plus, the One who gave me His life, even allowed me to be graced with being pregnant, a gift I did not feel could or would ever happen to me, because of such trauma in my past. I had not dealt with or faced the pregnancy and my previous loss or the trauma, which caused me to conceive back then, in the first place, so this pregnancy was a way for me to actually 'feel' again! My emotions were numb most of the time before this ever since the last painful experiences I had gone through.

They decided to send me to have an ultrasound to find out where and what was happening within my womb. When I got downstairs, the radiographer panicked, whilst I could see the images of my baby boy on screen kicking about and peacefully enjoying the warmth of his mother's protection. She ran outside of the room and rang the ward to let them know that I was giving birth right there and then. I was not, but she saw how low my little one was and he was engaged in my pelvis. Hence the agony I kept finding myself in, when I would walk or sit or do much of anything, except lay down.

Whilst I was there, still staring at the screen, I saw hands located within my womb, in the formation of praying hands, they were covering the exit of my womb, I felt like God Himself was telling me "*everything was going to be okay*!" I turned and told my mum, who saw the hands at the time, but she cannot remember this now, so at times it seems now like a figment of my imagination, but I KNOW what I saw and it will forever be etched in my memory! I told her "*God's got Kiana in His hands*!"

The name Kiana Ayani was what I was going to name my baby and I believed all along that I would be giving birth to a baby girl. The meanings became even more real to me following my baby's arrival, because little did I know, that despite me carrying a baby boy, this child was in actual fact a physical manifestation of the name's meanings "*Divine, Heavenly*," "*A Gift of God*" and my "*Beautiful Flower*" and that was where my healing lay.

I was immediately rushed back to the pre-natal unit, Aunty Carole had come that day, she sat opposite my bed and I recall having yet more bloods taken with more visits from the consultant paediatrician examining me and telling me, with such urgency in her voice that I needed to terminate. I told her blatantly, "Jesus gave me His life, so if I must die, to save this child, then so be it! My mum and my brother will look after him!" I no longer felt afraid, my room was filled with such peace and the doctors looked at me in awe, speechless. Their words and pleading of no effect to my decision and choice to proceed with my dangerous pregnancy, no matter what, because I was filled up with the Word of God! Later on, I recall being told by Aunty Carole, that she "*had never seen such faith*!" I can truly say that I was filled with such inner peace, despite how bad the situation and pain looked.

The following scripture was all that filled my mind, heart and soul;

"No one has greater love [nor stronger commitment] than to lay down his own life for his friend."

John 15:9 (AMP)

This seemed to be my battle, the remainder of the week. The care or rather, lack of was shocking. I was left to shower unaided, with the exception of my mum to help me, but no commode or chair was provided, given the fact that my bed was soaked with the amount of blood I was losing on a daily basis, I was so ghastly pale and I recall standing in the shower, almost blacking out. I saw dots and speckles all around me and quickly my mum reached out to support me getting out of the shower. I somehow managed to be filled up with joy, but we did let the nurses know that I was still losing so much blood.

They seemed oblivious of this fact, despite constantly changing my bedding due to how much I was losing daily, I was kept on an intravenous drip. At times they would change my bedding multiple times throughout the day. The final few days were much the same. I recall being checked by a nurse, who then proceeded to open the door with my blood smeared on her gloves. To my horror, she did not change her gloves, as she exited my room into the corridor.

So finally, the morning where my baby was coming. I recall my cervix being fully dilated, yet my waters did not break, so unlike the last time, nobody rushed to be at my side. I just kept having contractions and somehow, we all just knew it was time for his arrival. It was the morning of February fifteenth, 2008 and it all happened so quickly. I remember it just being myself, my mum and this midwife, with blonde shoulder length hair. She kept closing her eyes, she said she was tired because she had a long night. Yet here my life and that of my unborn child was completely in her hands. I had fought with every ounce of will power within me to hold him inside my womb till medically there was a chance for him to be deemed 'viable', which he now was. I was five full months' pregnant and he was one day short of twenty-weeks gestationally. I began pushing, whilst turned on all fours, I found it much easier in this position. My head buried in a pillow and roaring like a lioness!!!

I felt a huge 'plop', looking down it was a massive lump of blood and from my previous delivery, I thought this was the placenta, but my baby had not yet come out of me, which confused me. Asking the midwife, who was holding a large metal bowl up, with this huge lump in her hands, what it was, she said placidly, "*it's just a blood clot*!" That was the largest blood clot I had ever seen! Yet I could not even take time off to look around, as not long after the blood clot fell from me, my baby decided to just fall out of me, as I continued pushing as hard as I could, with every contraction.

Josiah Azaniah Hakim was born at seven-fifteen AM. When I looked over at the midwife, she quickly picked up my baby boy, who was alive and still encased within his blood-filled amniotic sac, whilst he was kicking away with those strong little legs. I watched how the midwife fought with a pair of surgical scissors to pierce a hole within this amniotic sac and then concluded in my mind, that they had just wanted my baby to die, hence the fear spreading when they told me about how they might rupture his sac by stitching my cervix closed. I felt that it was so that they would not have to worry about another baby being kept on life support, which costs a fortune and takes a lot of medical effort, because from what I saw my little one was a fighter, just as strong as his mama and grandma and the long line of strong Zambian women who came before us!

The midwife wrapped the tiniest living baby I have ever been so close to, in my hands in a really rough towel and to my surprise he was breathing. He weighed just two hundred and seventy-five grams and he was long. Although his eyes were still tightly closed, his nose and mouth were moist, as he kept turning his neck and gasping for air, but no audible sound could be heard; he was perfect! I guess I was just left to have his final moments with my mum and Aunty JackJack, who was my beautiful heaven-sent mama, who helped me through the difficult patch my mum and I had gone through. We were so close and she was my lifeline and we spent many days and nights enjoying aunty and niece trips prior to this and after. Another midwife came in the room and held Josiah, before he eventually breathed his last. She appeared especially amused when she stated, "*he is actually a bonnie baby and he is strong*!" His little finger grasped my index finger, whilst squeezing and he turned and lifted his head, gasping for air, whilst his little heart pumped ever so fast, visibly within his chest wall. With that she walked away and the rest that followed was just a blur, except he lived two hours and fifteen minutes before gasping with his last breath. I was worn out totally. I was not checked or examined before leaving that ward. Surreal it was indeed!

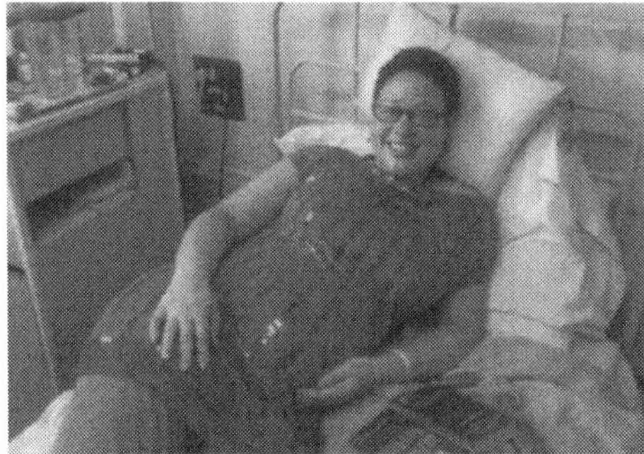

14th February 2008 – Valentines' Day – Pre-Natal Unit I had lost so much blood by this time, weak, but my blood levels had not been checked, yet still expecting a miracle, at peace and always smiling. I had briefly blacked out in the shower on this day, my mum had to help me shower and get back to bed.

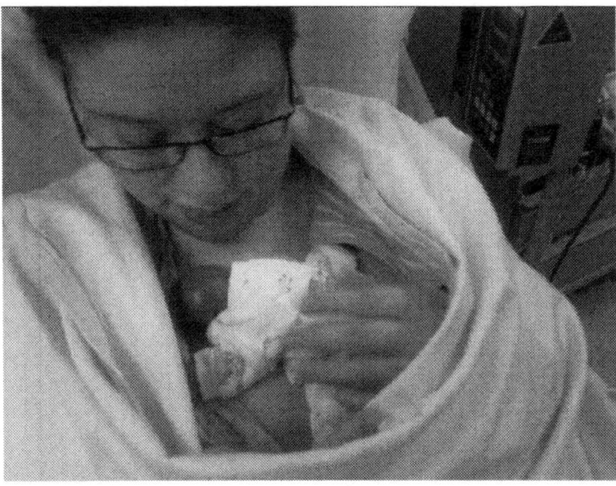

15th February 2008 - My precious baby boy was born, fought for his little life for two hours and fifteen minutes and died in my arms. He had breathed his last by this time. I was not given any examination, nor medical aid, so left the ward, just hours after delivering my little one, to go home with such complications and pain until my midwife came and booked me in for urgent tests a week later, panicking at my severe 1300ml blood loss.

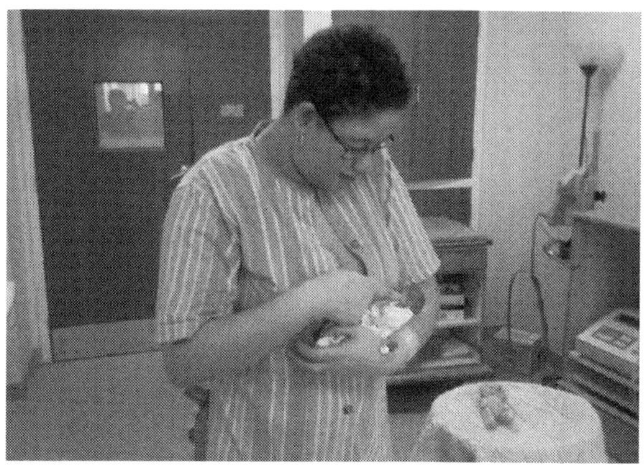

15th February 2008 – I honestly believed he was coming home with me, the reality of everything which was happening had not begun to sink in.

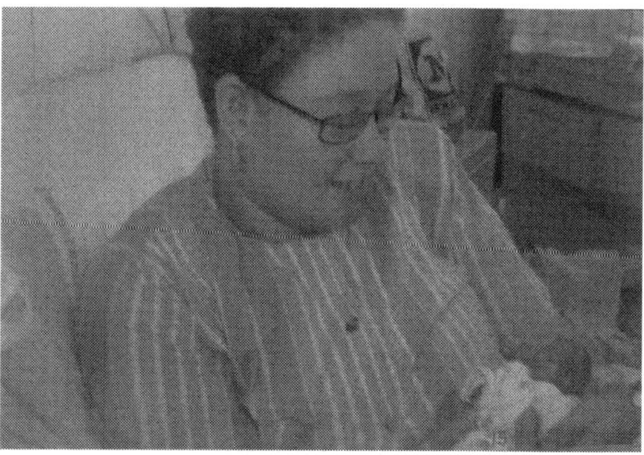

I was so overjoyed at having my baby boy in my arms, despite the pain I was in and how exhausted I felt at this time. I recall mum continuously praying in the room around me. The midwife had already left the room at this point.

I was allowed to have a family room, a couple of hours later, where close family and friends were allowed to visit and pay their respects and see my precious little one. He was as much theirs as he was mine! I was totally exhausted and holding my emotions together, I do not know how though, as everyone else around me was sobbing! I just could not.

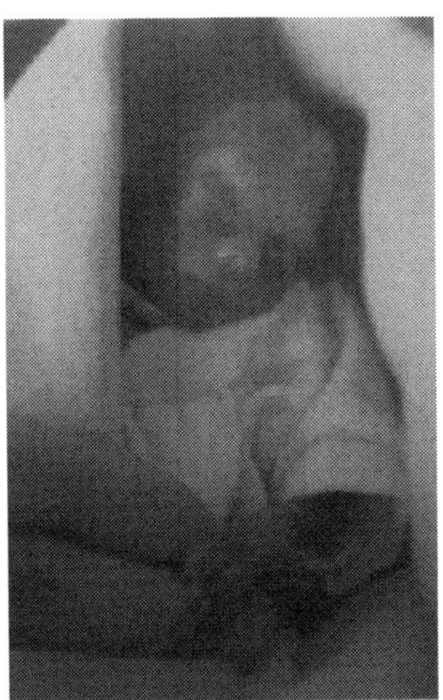

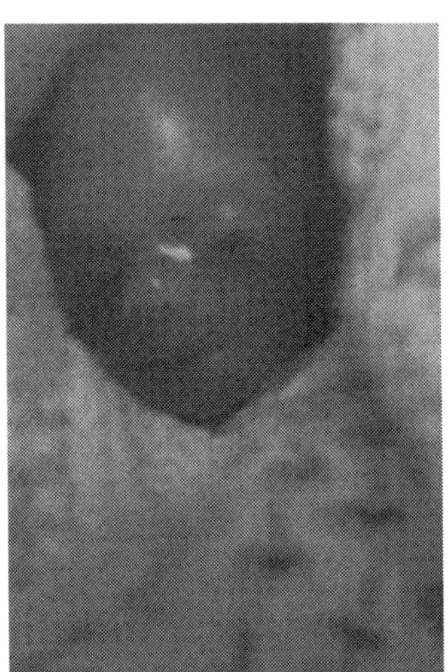

Josiah's whole hand fit into one of my fingers and he held my hand and squeezed, as gentle as it was, I felt he wanted me to know it was okay to let him go.

It was not until a week later, where my community midwife, Sister Prudames, who was wonderful came to do a home visit. She received an urgent telephone call when she was conducting my visit and immediately in shocked high-pitched tones responded "*what? That's too low*", as she was given my blood count. My haemoglobin levels were very low. They were lower than 8, I only found that out this past December, after finally speaking to my haematologist, something I did not even think to get informed of ever before. I found out I lost just under two and a half pints of blood that whole week. As I was walking to the GP, I began having those stabbing pubic bone pains, walking in the street and doubling over grabbing my groin was an embarrassing experience, but I could not stop myself, because this was agony. This continued along with debilitating back pains, for months following my traumatic delivery.

I actually wrote a seven-page complaint letter to the Hospital Ombudsman at the time, following my discharge and looked into having my own lawyer to proceed with a negligence claim, but continued having such complications that my body and mind were totally consumed with all the pain and grief, so I could not go ahead with that. However, I did see an article about another child, who was at that time, five years old following being born at five months gestationally and had no brain damage or other complications, that they usually notify the parents they would most certainly have. This was just a few days following my baby boy Josiah Azaniah Hakim's funeral. That drove me deeper into despair and I suffered with 'silent' depression for many years following this period of my life.

He was my little Valentine! The best gift anyone could have ever given me! Later that year, after securing a job, I recall having severe episodes of stabbing pubic bone and back pains, not realizing I was having crisis pains because I just did not connect the dots. I only knew the usual crisis pains being accompanied with fevers and swelling of my hands and arms and the pain spreading throughout my whole body. Yet this past year 2020, I now know for definite what was wrong with me back then, even following delivery.

I was off work quite a lot and could not cope with the pain I was in. I eventually felt that I was going to die internally; both emotionally due to the unhealthy relationship my late child's father and I had and spiritually I felt dead already and needed a change of scenery and because of that, I had to move out of Leeds. Although we briefly broke up, we often would part ways and then things would go back to how they previously were. I just could not let go, nor could he until much later in my later twenties.

I did move and still those pains kept occurring for the duration of my studies and working life whilst I was living in Manchester. I continued to have really bad episodes of crisis pains mostly within my limbs and whenever I got infections, I was out of action completely for approximately two to eight weeks at a time every single time. I ended up on disciplinary action once, if only I had medical evidence and been given the appropriate attention all those years ago, I would have at least had a leg to stand on within my career.

Reading the poem I wrote for my baby boy, with my baby cousin-sister Ruby by my side - Josiah's funeral – 5th March 2008

My beautiful big sister and dearest friend, Kathryn sang so beautifully at Josiah's funeral service. We requested everyone to not specifically dress in all-black attire, despite it being a sad occasion, we wanted to celebrate that mum and I were gifted with seeing him alive, however brief and that I was still alive!

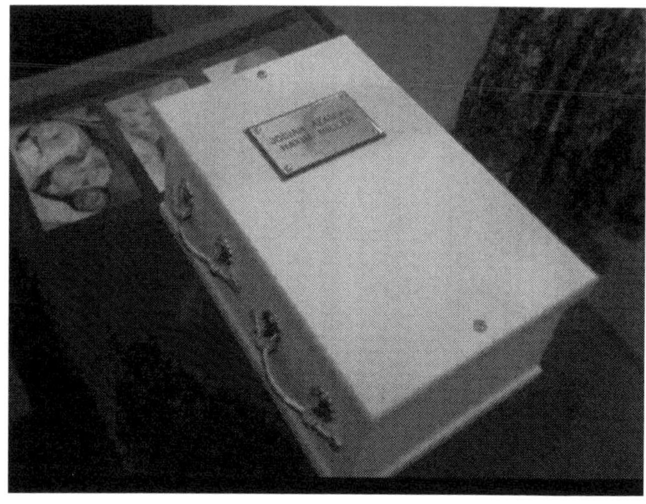

We laid my little one to rest 5th March 2008 and said our final goodbyes.

The Lord comforted me through the following passages of scripture through this painful time of grief.

" 1 Josiah was eight years old when he became king, and reigned for thirty-one years in Jerusalem. His mother's name was Jedidah daughter of Adaiah of Bozkath.

2 He did what was right in the sight of the Lord and walked in all the ways of his father (ancestor) David and did not turn aside to the right or to the left."
2 Kings 22: 1-2 (AMP)

" Before him there was no king like Josiah who turned to the Lord with all his heart and all his soul and all his might, in accordance with all the Law of Moses; nor did anyone like him arise after him."
2 Kings 23:25 (AMP)

CHAPTER 9.
PYELONEPHRITIS – BLACKING OUT AT THE GYM

Anyone who knows me, remembers me as a very active person. An avid gym goer and a keen runner. I would always need to hydrate extremely well and because of that, urinate often and at times would struggle with breathlessness and catching my breath when working out hard, but I never had any other major problems, until hitting 2014.

I was having flank pain on the left-hand side and feeling extremely nauseous, especially when I would lay down to sleep. However, I was out of work at the time and did not have the money to travel in and out of town on a regular basis. I had been having this pain for some time, but my doctor's surgery was on the other side of town.

Since moving into my studio apartment, in the November of 2013, after moving out of my exes home, I was waiting for my new locum contract to come through, but it did not, so I was waiting and had signed on to receive Job Seeker's Allowance, so that I would still be getting some form of income.

My usual regime began with very early mornings when I was out of work and taking time out to heal from a period of stress, which affected my blood pressure and causing me headaches similar to those of last year. I was not overweight, in fact, quite the opposite. I was very slim and running daily at least five miles; two and a half into town and the same on the journey back. I would also train for hours in the gym and then when I got home, I would spend a whole heap of time in worship. Basking in God's presence was what I longed for. I had come out of a very stressful situation and my ex of just under eight years and I had broken up. For good this time! I needed to get out of there, it was slowly killing me inside with the unhealthy way things were!

Please note I no longer held, nor do I hold any hard feelings towards him. I realised he was hurting just as much as I was and I had come to realise that hurting people, hurt people. I had to learn to forgive myself and when I did that and accepted the Lord's total and absolute gift of love, I then was able to forgive him totally and let go entirely! After all, I loved him and he gave me the most precious gift any human being could give another, my beautiful baby boy! I also realised it just was not the right time for us to be together. He needed to heal and forgive himself too, no matter how ready I was for us to heal together.

My healing did not happen overnight, it took some time, but forgiveness is a process and confession brings possession, of those very things we declare aloud and consistently over our lives. This I did and within 6 months I was totally free from bitterness and felt release in the way I began loving myself, because the Lord taught me personally how to love me, by teaching me how to love Him first. Something I wish I had known to do much earlier, instead of carrying all this hurt and trauma around for the past seventeen years!

Anyway, this one day stands out more than any other, because this was something potentially serious, had I not bothered to go to the A&E, like I almost decided not to.

I was in the middle of being my usual competitive self during an early morning gym class. I think I was doing cardio circuit training; I believe I had done two or three other classes beforehand and was well hydrated as per usual, I always got so thirsty, so since childhood drank more than anyone else that I knew.

All of a sudden, I got really dizzy and the room began spinning and I saw black dots everywhere and fell over and briefly blacked out. My friend and personal trainer were gathered around me so fast checking that I was okay. I was made to sit out for approximately thirty minutes and then went to an appointment that I had, with the job centre in Leeds city centre before making my way reluctantly to the hospital A&E.

After my observations and urine samples were taken, I was told that it was a good job I went in when I did. There was an infection in my kidneys, which could have caused sepsis and ultimately kidney damage and I needed antibiotics via drip form. I was told that I would have gone comatose if I had waited any longer and that I had pyelonephritis.

I was allowed to return home to sleep that night, but had to go back to the hospital to have more antibiotics via drip form for the coming next few days. Thankfully, after the medication was given to me, I have not suffered with pyelonephritis again. I am extremely conscious of hydrating during exercise, although I thought I was before, I am even more diligent in doing so now.

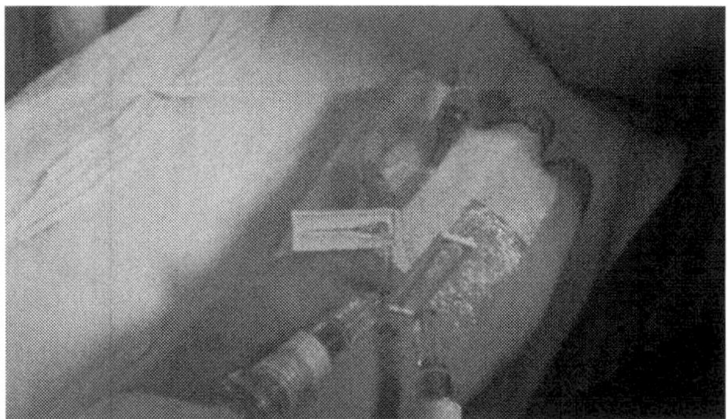

24th April 2014 – Admitted to hospital and put on fluids and antibiotics via drip for the day and the next few days in day clinics.

CHAPTER 10.
I CAN'T MOVE…BAD BACK

As I earlier mentioned another thing I have come to realise is that back pain, which I have often suffered with growing up and especially following my pregnancy is common with sickle cell trait and other sickled haemoglobinopathy disorders. I did not know just how much this would affect me though, until experiencing this extremely severe crisis.

During the early months of 2017, I had undergone a very stressful period, where I was running my business from my new home, which I rented with my mum. My landlords of the place where I had been living from 2013 in Beeston, Leeds, following moving out of my ex-boyfriend's home had made a mistake with my rent payments, to which they later apologized for. However, they had already threatened me in 2015, stating that I had not paid them and told me that they would kick me out. I then began noticing that upon returning home from my shop premises my door kept being opened, so I felt that someone had been searching through my personal things and considering the place was a tiny studio flat and often housed very strange and I would say, not very nice characters, (not making judgements, but I had a few run-ins with domestically violent or drugged up neighbours beating up their girlfriends or banging on my door whilst my niece and I slept in the middle of the night). I felt it was time to move on rather than be kicked out. So I handed in my notice and moved in with my sister-in-law and niece, whilst continuing to run my shop from the Sugar Mills, where I had rented a room to carry out my therapy work professionally.

I worked at the Sugar Mills until I could not afford to rent the room, again due to falling ill, so I was unable to work for a couple of weeks (a thing I could not afford to do at that time, although I was bringing in a steady income by then) and then in 2016, mum and I were offered a property together. This was not a long wait. Mum had been staying at my brother's place in his room, whilst he stayed on his sofa. This was definitely not ideal, as the place was only one bedroomed and I would share my time between crashing at his place and crashing at my sister-in-law's. At my brother's we often had my niece stay over, she was six years of age at this time, so it was rather cramped most of the time. Not to mention, my whole house had been reduced to cardboard boxes and suitcases, including the sentimental items my mum had kept, from our big house move, all those years ago from Chapeltown, when I had moved to Manchester and mum had moved out of Leeds to go and volunteer as a cook, cleaner, seamstress and child minder in Holland at Cornerstones Intercultural Bible College. So, you can imagine just how cramped this new, albeit temporary living arrangement was.

So, in April 2016 when we were offered our very own space; a two bedroomed council flat, we gladly accepted. I made the living room my therapy room and continued running things from there.

Since moving into our own place though, finances were tough and my business had suffered since moving from my shop premises into working from the tower block of flats we moved into. It was not an ideal location at all and since I had suffered a back injury in 2015 at the gym, whilst deadlifting quite heavy (eighty-five kilograms) without a back support belt. Considering the doctors could not tell me what this was, although they suspected it to be a slipped disc, but there was later found to be no evidence of this, from other doctors, my chiropractor and my physiotherapist stated this was not the case either. I now believe that my body was just injured and taking additional time to heal itself, which worsened because of my trait status, as is always the case whenever I fall ill.

So, working fulltime within the week as a band four associate practitioner, of which I had trained in during my time in Manchester and become qualified for, whilst carrying out holistic therapies and non-surgical aesthetics during evenings and weekends and with cooking and cleaning on evenings began to become overwhelming on my body. Not to mention the stress I felt, with my mum falling really sick and for the first time in my whole entire life, she was hospitalised on my birthday in 2016, which just got too much to cope with physically for me.

My brother then ended up having a knee operation in February 2017, which ended up with us visiting him immediately following his surgery and witnessing him taking a really bad turn directly in front of my mum, myself and my niece, who was so frightened seeing her daddy like that. An image I also am not likely to forget anytime soon.

It is no wonder I ended up collapsing in histopathology department of the lab where I worked in February 2017 and my doctor colleagues within pathology examined and sent me home due to exhaustion. I never returned!

My rest period, turned into months of agony. I slept for initially just two weeks and then one morning, I could not lift anything below my shoulders up from the bed. I recall this being the worst my back has ever been. At one stage I called for an ambulance to check my legs for paralysis, at one point, because I could not move them. I began using my brother's crutches to manoeuvre around from my bed to the toilet, then sliding my back down the wall, so I was sitting against the wall and leaning on my crutch to move to the toilet and lowered myself. Cleaning myself was almost impossible, as I could not turn in the slightest. Thankfully, I was able to use a squirt bottle to wash myself or at the worst times ask my mother for help to clean me. My mum also had to bathe me and assist me with getting dressed on my lower half of my body.

It took me over eight months of massage therapy and somehow attending college, where I obtained my higher Level two ITEC diplomas in Complementary Therapies and Level three ITEC diplomas in Indian Head and Massage Therapies. I clearly recall the ladies on my course asking me whether I should be there on the first day of college, due to being unable to bend to pick up my pen, which fell to the floor during registration. Someone had to do that for me and my mum being the darling she always has been, patiently accompanied me to and from college, where she wheeled my trolley case with my towels and books and study essentials every week, until I regained more strength.

I mention the above in regards to my back being so affected, as the spasms in my muscles are very similar to what I have been experiencing during this past year and ongoing on a regular basis. Stress was what brought on that pain and all I could do was sleep for days following having deep tissue massages at college. I did become mobile and able to carry out massage therapy on colleagues and within my business after months' of having such deep tissue massages myself. It would knock me for six. Anyone who has trained in detox therapy, knows that massage is a great toxin release and detox for the body. All detox therapy drains the body and inflammation is a sign of toxin build up. Stress causes toxin build up and can take a while to remove. I know that due to the immense physical, emotional and mental stress I had been going through at this time, my body just had enough, hence it once again gave up on me.

After hearing other sickle cell warriors stories, I have heard that the back pain they go through is also intense and looking back, since my childhood I often had back problems. Considering all the medics I saw stated that my back had not sustained a slipped disc and I had not pulled a muscle, although I did end up with sciatica (trapped nerve), at one stage which was different to the agony that specific points in my back felt.

The sciatica has totally gone to this day, thank God, but even now, at times I cannot move at all and I know why. This back pain comes and goes whenever I have these painful episodes playing up, so I still keep a crutch nearby just incase!

CHAPTER 11.
SURGERY – NOT ENOUGH OXYGEN

During the majority of the year 2018 and in 2019, I had been having menorrhagia or intermittent bleeding between my periods. This was not quite the same as a period, but I would have what seemed like a discharge of blood or spotting quite often. I had been on the combined contraceptive pill for years, to control my abnormal periods, but then was told that this needed to change to the progesterone only pill, due to the risks of stroke because of my ethnicity, being overweight and because I have a family history of high blood pressure and strokes. I changed and things seemed to get increasingly worse.

Eventually I was checked out by a Gynaecologist and had a hysteroscopy examination done to see what was going on within my womb. Even though I had worked in a clinical laboratory and received and assisted within lab cut ups, where the consultant Pathologist or Biomedical scientist would dissect surgical specimens; some of which included uterus, prostate, breast tissue or total mastectomies, biopsies, kidneys, liver, gall bladder, gastrointestinal specimens too and other surgical and skin specimens, you would have thought that I would be used to seeing polyps. After all, I did this for over five years, but it was a total shock to me when I asked to be shown the screen and saw that my uterus was filled to the brim with large, ugly polyps. I could not see any normal looking tissue at all.

Because of the pain that just having a camera inserted into my uterus in the day clinic caused me to be in, I was told I would need to have my womb scraped and cauterised and a D and C (dilate and curettage).

So, they got me ready for pre-op and within a couple of weeks I was admitted into hospital for this day surgery under general anaesthetic. I had told all the pre-operation staff involved in my care repeatedly of my status as a symptomatic sickle cell trait patient and advised them of my allergies to amoxycillin in drip form, which had occurred when I was in hospital previously with pneumonia.

Again, I told the day staff on the ward I was in that I had sickle cell trait and thought that was enough. My mum and I had worn our winter puffer coats, due to it being October 2019 and quite chilly already. I am so glad I always wrap up and did that particular day, as I did not know what relief my coat would bring after my surgery, though it did not prevent me becoming really sick.

I remember being wheeled into the theatre and having an injection filled with anasthetic injected into the canula in my left hand, literally on the inside of my wrist and the next moment I was waking up immediately after surgery, feeling super cold with a dry mouth. I was so thirsty. That was such an awful feeling of having to be intubated and my throat felt sore with the scratching of the tube which was inserted down it.

Upon arriving at the bay where I had left my mum prior to surgery, I asked for another blanket, to which I was given a warm one. That felt so nice, as my body felt like there was ice water flowing through my veins. I looked at my mum and said to her "*I'm going to get sick, I am really, really cold!*" I knew what was going to follow, because I had been here before and I know my body well. This always frightened me, because I have mental images stuck in my head of how bad my crisis pains were in the past, when they come, because they were not as often as they used to be, they are still always severe and keep me unable to function or do anything when I am in a severe crisis.

My mum gave me her puffer coat and she also laid my puffer coat on top of me. We did again ask the nurses for yet another blanket, because I could feel a cold vent above me, blowing out cool air, I stressed to them, "*I have sickle cell trait and I am very cold!*" I told them I am symptomatic and have been throughout the years, so the cold was a trigger for me. Yet I was informed that they had run out of blankets on that ward, because the laundry had not as yet been delivered. Gosh, if only they knew just what the lack of preventative measures available to me then later caused!

Thinking back, as I write this chapter, the repercussions for them could have been quite serious, if I had decided to pursue medical negligence claims for each time that something went wrong with my health due to being ignored or fobbed off or not believed, because I took notes and had taken pictures of everything, as I do now. I always have documented and journaled, since my teenage years and kept quite detailed records too, but now I take photographic evidence of everything, just in case.

Approximately five hours after being on the ward, perhaps two hours after surgery, I was allowed to eat something and have a hot cup of tea. The nausea I felt was so overwhelming, the effects of the anasthetic were still very much present. Still, I was allowed to go home that day, as we would call a taxi or my friend, who drove if she was able to collect us. She was, so she dropped us off at home at around three PM Greenwich Mean Time (GMT).

Well, what a horrible recovery period I had. So, I bled continuously for over four weeks, with full blown crisis pain symptoms and stabbing pubic bone pains by the time I got home and got into bed. This was only eight hours since being admitted onto the ward and approximately one to two hours since being discharged from the ward. I began feeling extremely nauseous, feverish and having stabbing pains in my thighs, arms and pubic bone and literally crawled on all fours to go to the toilet later that evening and the tears and screaming out in pain was unbearable for my poor mum to have to wait on and nurse me.

I remember telling the advanced nurse practitioner (ANP) who saw me at my doctor's surgery that I carry sickle cell trait, I could not sit down properly and remember clearly rocking myself back and forth, sitting balanced on the edge of the chair in the waiting room and in her office. She totally ignored me and said flippantly, "*you just have a bit of a cold, that's all!*" Wow! Often at times, I really have wished that these ignorant doctors and nurses would experience just a little taste of what I have so often gone through, just to see how they would handle it, because I know just how much I have had to fight and almost died in doing so!

I pray that each and every one of them involved in my care over the years has gone and done further research into sickle cell trait and read up on the complications I now have heard many other symptomatic carriers experience and the pains they have lived with all their lives, but have been ignored or made to feel so small and insignificant because of the lack of medical knowledge that there is out there! I know that it is not the Godly thing to wish upon anyone and I do not wish them any harm, but I wish they knew just what unnecessary trauma they have caused so many of us over the years. I forgive them now, but at the time, I wished they could feel just a tiny taste of what I felt!

I kept having to make appointments on a weekly basis, as a surgery so minor, should not have caused me so much pain in my pubic bone, nor made me super unwell. The ANP was still insisting that I had a cold, until I told her I was having stabbing bones and kept having to repeat myself, explaining I had a fever and chills and stabbing spine pains too. I finally agreed to her putting it down to the flu, as so many episodes of illness I had done so because of how I had been disbelieved and belittled. I detest and absolutely hate going to the doctors and at times have thought I would rather die than go to see a doctor, a stance my mother takes to this day, because of her many poor experiences! How sad, that the ones we entrust with our care, we cannot really trust to care for us, until something bad happens! I plan on sending a copy of this chapter to my GP surgery wrapped as a present to that very nurse, she knows just who she is, but I feel a little cheeky. However, backed up with medical re-education I believe this would not go amiss and could be the life or death of someone else less able to cope--both physically and mentally-- than I am!

At one point she examined my stomach, to rule out anything sinister, because of the pains I was having continually, until week four and then things returned back to normal, even though the pain continued, not as often as it had been doing so before.

21st October 2019 – prior to minor surgery under general anasthetic

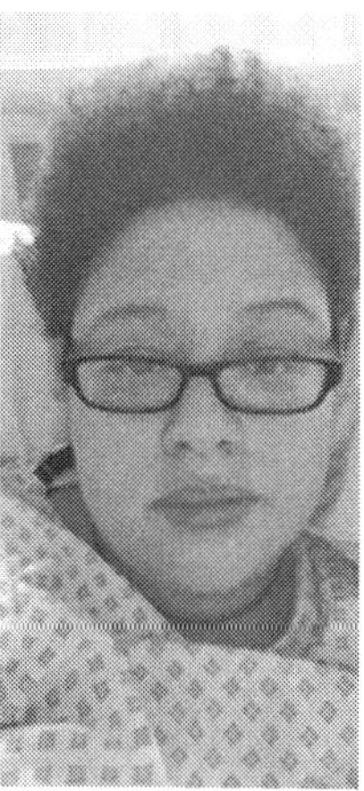

Back on the ward after my procedure

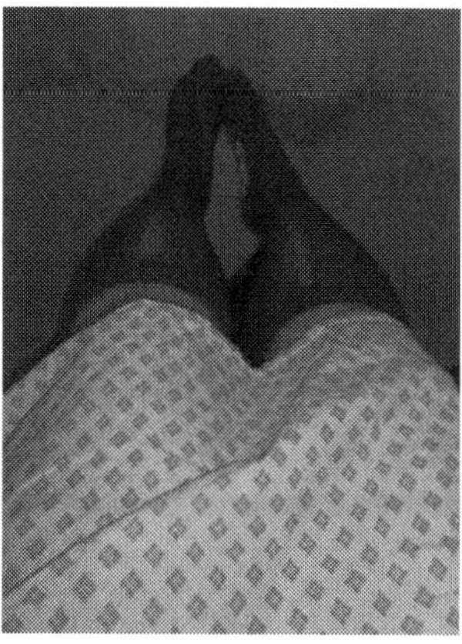

DVT Stockings given to me pre-surgery to prevent blood clots

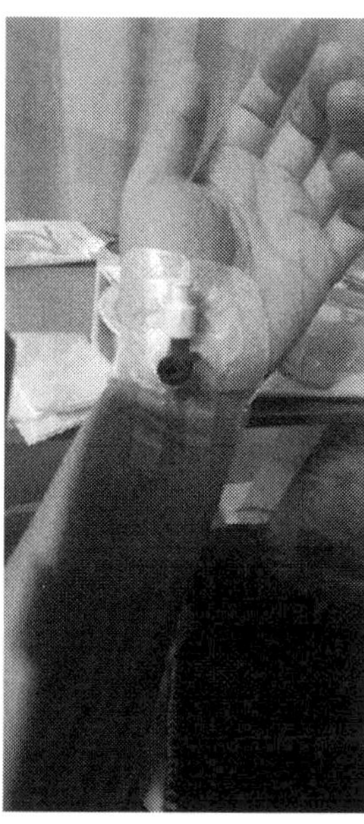

21st October 2019 – just before being hooked up to an ice-cold drip.

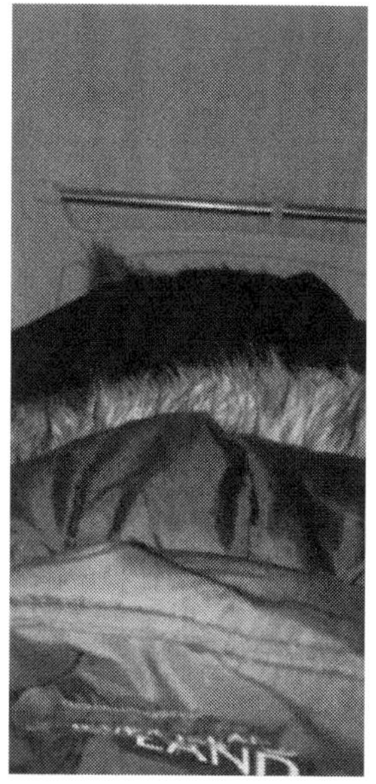

Both mine and my mum's puffer coats on top of me, despite me requesting more blankets.

30th October 2019 in so much pain with fever and flu type symptoms and pubic bone crisis pains as per my usual symptoms, stomach swelling

CHAPTER 12.
HOSPITAL ADMISSION – I'VE HAD A STROKE ?BELLS PALSY

This was the first time I had ever been in hospital on my own, without my mum being present or being allowed to visit. I clearly recall the pounding headaches I had been having since March 2020, which progressively worsened over the year. When I suffered the severe crisis pains from June to September 2020, I did have continual headaches. However, following this period of time, I began suffering really severely debilitating headaches again. The crisis pains continued, along with a menstrual cycle which did not want to disappear from September 2020 until January 2021. Things seemed to be going backwards. I had been waiting for a referral to Neurology to come through after having to push them from the end of July, as no one at my Family Doctor's surgery believed me as to what was going on with limb weakness accompanied with pounding headaches and I was told too many of my body's systems were involved for them to investigate one specific problem. From what I had read up on, I knew that silent strokes were often a symptom of sickle cell and could prove to be fatal if left untreated. So, I kept insisting on an urgent referral. My referral finally came through in December, where I was able to discuss with my neurologist consultant the severity of the headaches.

These pounding headaches had worsened and I had been having crisis pains in my head, from June onwards, on the left-hand side, above my ear. They would come on especially at nighttime and be that bad at times, they were felt from my collar bone, all the way up into my neck and would be stabbing like in presentation. Along with these stabbing pains, when my head began to pound, it felt like such pressure over my left eye socket and it made me dizzy, lose my vision to the point where I was walking into walls and doors when waking up to go to the toilet at night. I felt so nauseous with these headaches and no amount of sleeping or hydration would relieve them. Neither would medication. My doctor had treated me for high blood pressure, in March 2020, after I attended the A&E department of my nearest hospital. There was a GP on site at the A&E, who had requested for me to have a CT scan right there and then, but when I got back to the nurses' station they refused and told me that my blood pressure was only slightly elevated and that I would need to go back to my GP for medication.

So, December arrived and the headaches suddenly changed from crisis head pains to now more increased throbbing along with stabbing pains in my neck and into the left part of my head. The headaches seemed to be continuous from the twelfth of December. I phoned into work leaving a voicemail message on Sunday late night stating that I was not able to attend work on Monday fourteenth December, because I could not see how I could function with feeling so ill. I managed to sign into work in the afternoon on Tuesday fifteenth after my haematology telephone appointment, but ended up in so much pain, feeling so nauseous, that my mum came in my office, because I was rocking back and forth, groaning so loudly, unable to see or to process any information, frequently going completely blank and not remembering what I was in the middle of doing. It took me an hour to notify my boss via email of exactly what was going on within my body and head especially. I just could not focus or think. My right arm was tingling and had pain whenever I touched it. It felt like it was being constricted along with severe crisis pains.

My mum told me to stop working when she saw how bad I looked, but I had felt quite pressured from my boss, as I had informed her of the way I was feeling and I was told that I would be better off using annual leave in oppose to taking off sick leave again, because I had over three full months sickness absences that year already. So, I felt torn and worried about my absences, but my health had to come first. I stopped working and went to the doctors' surgery to have my blood tests taken at three PM that day too, because I had notified my GP of my continual blood loss with huge clots measuring approximately ten to fourteen inches long and approximately four centimetres in thickness. These had become the normal everyday occurrence. I would feel like the bleeding was stopping and all of a sudden, later in the day I would get an overwhelming gushing feeling and I would rush to the toilet to check I was okay and to ensure I had not messed myself and noticed how heavy my flow was.

At one point, I was wearing what my niece had once called lady nappies, Tena lady pads, because of their length and thickness and the amount of protection they provided. Often though I leaked outside them, because they would become so filled. No matter if I wore two pads at a time and changed up to four times a day. I must say how grateful I am to Tena Lady for those humongous ugly things, as lady nappies or not, they were the only pads keeping me from embarrassment when my brother would come to assist my mum and I, who were both very unwell. He often had to cook or to clean or to help in whatever way we needed, when he was off work. My mum had been very weak and ill and I do feel the toll of being a full-time carer to me when I was so unwell, began to take full effect on her health even more so. As we both needed that help, he was our support bubble.

Later on, the evening of December fifteenth, I felt like my right cheek had moved into my right eye. It felt like my lip had become numb and I was smiling crooked. I asked my brother who was sat opposite me, at the other end of the room, whether he noticed if my face was lopsided. He stated he did not notice anything. So, I ignored it and went to bed around ten PM. My mum and I tend to sleep next to each other, if we are feeling unwell, just because at times, it has been absolutely necessary. When I have been in too much pain to lift myself off from where I lay or vice versa, when my mum has been too weak to even lift her head off her pillow, so knowing how bad I had been feeling, my mum slept in my room to be there if I needed her that night.

Around midnight, I decided to get up from where I lay trying to get comfortable and began crying because the pain was so unbearable. I did not want to wake my sleeping mother, so I went to the kitchen and took my phone and texted my friend. She was always awake at this time. We ended up speaking over voice messages, because I could hardly see and I told her how bad this pain was. I told her that maybe I was hungry, as I had not eaten earlier that evening due to the amount of pain I was in, so I made a quick sandwich. However, I told her that it felt very strange when I tried to open my mouth to take a bite. I could not get my mouth to open properly, it felt numb, as if I had been to the dentist and my arm still felt painful. I still could not see properly. We chatted for about ten minutes and then I told her I was going to go sit in the living room to try make myself tired, because the pain got unbearable. I took codeine, which was what I had been prescribed, although this did not touch anything at all. It had never helped me, as my body over the years had become used to strong medication, which I took only when I was in desperate need of it. Otherwise, I tried to hydrate, take herbal remedies or alternative therapies and avoid pharmaceutical medication where possible, yet here I desperately was, in need of help. I finally got tired enough to sleep, so I went back to bed at approximately two AM on Wednesday sixteenth of December 2020, waking up later that morning at around eleven AM. I did not feel the intense pain which I had felt the day before at this time, although my mouth still felt numb, so my mum made me a bite to eat and off I went to go and brush my teeth.

I did not feel anything different with my body function, until I tried to grasp my toothbrush tightly with my right hand. I am right-handed and yet my fingers would not bend, close nor could I move my arm in a brushing motion. My arm felt very limp and then I began brushing my teeth as best as I could, with my left hand. As my right arm had been presenting with weakness the whole year since being in crisis from June, on and off, I thought it to be one of those times. When I tried to spit my toothpaste out of my mouth, it felt weird. I could not form an 'O' shape nor carry out the motion. The sound I made when spitting was not normal. I raised my head and looked in the mirror and the shock horror I felt when I realized that my face had dropped, was immense, I screamed, "mum I think I've had a stroke!" My mum ran to the bathroom and I showed her my face, to her horror, she then burst out laughing in shock and then burst into tears. This was scary!

She began praying aloud and I took a video and posted it to Facebook, for evidence just in case anything happened to me. I then rang my brother and sister-in-law to notify them of what had occurred and told them that mum might need their help, as I was going to ring for an ambulance. To all our surprise, the NHS operator on the phone, when I called for an ambulance, mentioned that an urgent call out was within two hours. So, I went to go and bath as quickly as I could. However, with bleeding and right limb weakness, it proved quite difficult, so my mum had to assist me. I felt out of my head with dizziness, but asked for my mum's help, as I feared falling or worse, drowning in the bath if I fell into the water filled tub.

It might seem really strange to you reading this now, but exactly a week prior to this, I had told my mum that I had an urgent feeling to get my hospital bag ready and my care plan. So, it was more or less packed and I just needed a few additional warm things just in case I was made to stay overnight.

When the ambulance came, they took me, my sickle cell trait file, which contained evidence of all my calls to my GP and included my care plan, which I had written up ready, with all the allergy info that medics might need highlighted should I end up unconscious and my overnight bag. The doctors in A&E were great! The doctor there was of Indian heritage and so I asked him if he saw many sickle cell trait patients coming through A&E in crisis or with other complications such as, I was in. He surprised me actually and said "yes, we get a lot, because we are a hospital, we cover a larger area within Leeds!" that was the first medic who mentioned yes when I asked whether any other sickle cell trait patients present in crisis or with other complications in relation to their sickle cell status.

I then was given a shot of morphine, which I cannot recall ever being given before with the exception of my first pregnancy and it took the pain almost instantly down to a bearable level. I felt a sudden release at the back of my neck, where it felt like my whole body had relaxed. I was then sent to have a CT scan. The doctors believed me to have had a mini stroke, due to the limb weakness and my presentation, but due to having a facial droop they then speculated whether it could have also been Bell's Palsy. A stroke nurse came and told me she believed I had suffered a mini stroke, because of my symptoms. I then was admitted to a Neurology admissions ward where major head and neck trauma cases were admitted following urgent surgery and the next morning a consultant neurologist came to visit with me and do some tests. By the beginning of the following week, I was given an MRI scan to check whether there was any significant brain damage. As my symptoms baffled all the consultants in charge of my care. I presented like I had a stroke, yet due to my facial droop, they assumed I had sustained a mild form of Bell's Palsy. I could not grip or use my right arm to function carrying out many tasks and my head felt as if it was floating above my body, albeit it feeling very heavy, let alone sitting on my shoulders. I required help to go as far as the bathroom to shower, because I was unsteady on my feet and extremely dizzy. I felt like I had something huge stuck inside my brain and not quite fully 'there', but it was the fact that my face just was not moving and by now I realized that it was the left side of my face which was abnormal.

On day two - when I had informed the consultant in charge of my care about the heavy bleeding I was experiencing and the placental type blood clots, which were extremely large in size and worrying me at this time, I told him that I had felt a firm blood clot at the back of my calf in the summertime, due to my limited mobility, which got him on his toes. He then prescribed me blood thinning injections into my tummy, to prevent any deep vein thrombosis or any pulmonary embolisms and other potential clots travelling up to my lungs and becoming fatal. I went on to explain the similarities when I was in labour for my second child. Due to the clotting and pain both times, I knew now that they were related to my sickle cell trait status and mentioning my status did seem to raise their alarm bells.

I could not understand how a facial droop signified Bell's Palsy, as my big Aunty suffered a stroke and her symptoms were exactly like mine. She woke the next day (some years ago now) feeling numb on the one side with a facial droop, which she did not notice until she tried to eat and the food spilled out of her mouth. This was the most embarrassing thing I have ever had happen to me too, because this was a fight against my own lips and tongue and it hurt when swallowing. She still has a slight facial droop to this day. So how could they tell me, who has a family history of strokes that I had not suffered one? My maternal grandfather, back in Zambia had suffered with two strokes, yet recovered fully and lived until the ripe old age of one-hundred and one years old, with his brain faculties intact and his memory as good as ever. Let me also state, I am still suffering with right arm limb weakness and stroke like symptoms to this day and it is early February now, as I finish writing of my horrific experiences!

Day four, I had an EMG electromyography test carried out, where needles are inserted into the muscles to ascertain damage and function. My whole right side was not functioning as it should, both my legs and my arms and fingers reflexes not responding to the pain properly, they were not moving and I had loss of grip function. Surely that should have told the doctors something!

Anyways in the need to focus on resting and staying positive, I made jokes with the nurses looking after me about my new face, looking like the '*Joker*' from Batman! I had some amazing friends who I hold extremely dear to my heart, bring some essentials from home and my Baji was my go-between and support bubble, travelling to and from my mums' and the hospital, taking my dirty clothes home and bringing me much needed Tena Lady pads.

In total, I was in hospital for nine days, although due to being moved constantly while in there with other head and neck and brain trauma patients, we collectively did not feel like we were getting much rest. This was mainly down to being up during the night with machines malfunctioning, if not in a lot of pain, or nurses frequenting the room to see to the beeping of equipment which had gone out of control, not quietly either, but rather noisily during the middle of the night. A few times, they would come rushing in the room talking loudly and attend to one patient or another elderly patient I rather took under my wing, she had early onset dementia. She had experienced a rather nasty fall and kept becoming extremely confused, as to why she was in hospital. She kept forgetting where she was and wondering whether her deceased husband had been telephoned to notify him of where she was. Often, she got up from her bed at night and would begin searching for her bag containing her purse, even after we all repeatedly informed her that it was not brought in with her and that the nurses would call her sister to look for it the next morning. My heart went out to so many lovely people I met on the bay I was in and we formed a little friendship bubble. This kept me going whilst I was alone in the ward, without my family and friends visiting to boost my spirits. I met some amazing staff, consisting of amazing nurses, sisters, healthcare assistants and auxiliary nurses! Some of whom, I will never forget! I was however looking forward to coming back home to just recoup, because I felt super lethargic, but I was afraid that due to being so exhausted whilst in hospital, I was going to suffer another crisis.

When I was moved for the fourth time within the same ward, I ended up in an area where it was freezing cold, so I really tried to take care of myself, wrapping up warmly, but my arm began swelling again, due to the cold combined with being too tired. I told the doctor who saw me the next morning and had to mention dactylitis (also known as hand and foot syndrome or swelling limbs), was a frequent symptom at the onset of all my previously suffered severe crisis, as he had no clue. I clearly recall him stating that "*sickle cell does not just present in one area; it is too generalized!*" To which, I heatedly replied, "*I know that, but that's how the onset of my crisis are!*" He did get his colleague to note that statement down. I so hoped and prayed that this was not another severe one, my body and mind could not cope with that!

I was later moved to another neurology ward L17, this was move number five, on the eighth night, twenty-third of December 2020, at approximately ten PM and the level of care I received whilst in there was of a very poor standard! I do remember though that the night staff did have more empathy and care than the day staff who took over on the following day shift, 24th December 2020. I was bleeding that heavily, that I had stained my bedding and had to lay on my bed the next morning, using the bath towel I was given to protect my clean clothes that I had freshly put on. This was not the same level of hygiene or care which I received whilst on the other ward I had just come from, L25.

Later that morning, the consultant came to see me and told me that I would be discharged so that I can be at home in comfort, whilst awaiting a Neck MRI scan to figure out what was going on in my neck, as they believed I could have also been suffering with possibly a trapped nerve and wanted to rule out any serious damage or clots. However, after suffering from sciatica and experiencing trapped nerve pain, for the majority of 2015 through to 2017, I know what that feels like and this just was not it! I was told that in some cases Bell's Palsy stays the way I was and in other cases it resolves itself. I was also told that it could come back. I was promised physiotherapy from the day I arrived on the ward, so informed the consultant that the physiotherapists had not once passed by to carry out any muscle strengthening rehabilitation techniques with me. Whilst being home I have still yet to be given physiotherapy.

As soon as I was given the okay to go home, a nurse asked whether I had anyone who was able to collect me and I told them my baji was able to do so later that day. I was then informed that they would telephone a taxi for me later, which ended up being within the next fifteen minutes. This did not give me sufficient time to pack all my belongings, as I was still very unsteady on my feet and my head was just spinning. So a nurse came and threw my things in my bags. The taxi did not take that long to arrive and a little nurse came to my bedside, somehow expecting me to walk and carry my bags, to which I informed her that I had a few bags and asked if she could assist me. This was the longest distance I had been expected to walk, in pain, since my admission into hospital. Off she half ran with my bags on a wheelchair, with me hobbling along. She had to keep stopping to wait for me to catch up to her, as I just could not keep up and needed to hold on to the walls from time to time to keep upright the whole way to the main hospital exit. No, LGI Ward L17 was really poor in its quality of care and its hygiene levels. I did cut my finger whilst utilising the toilet/shower room quite deeply, in the early hours of the morning and despite me asking for a dressing and reporting this deep gash, no one came to assist me to clean it, considering the state I was in. I wish I had told them I would datix both that cut and the poor hygiene I experienced whilst in their care - (datix is the hospital's in-house system of accident and incident reporting) - I wonder what they would have said then.

When I called my GP following my discharge, asking for a referral to the home help team, because my discharge summary note states ?Bell's Palsy with right sided limb weakness, my GP immediately said that my symptoms were affecting too many systems and told me that I could not apply for home help. I persisted with this though and I am still awaiting for those referrals for home help, because I cannot lift myself out of the bath, nor can I grip the bath handles or hold anything properly. I have almost fallen over in the bath on many occasions, due to not having the appropriate safety measures in place, at present.

My brain still feels foggy and I feel as if there is a film covering the posterior section of my brain on the right-hand side. My thoughts are not clear and it feels like even with the things that I know the answers to, I really have to think to respond or that I am not quite physically or mentally present. I do not somehow feel like myself.

I know to many, this description may not make sense, but I feel that something does not feel quite right in my brain. Science does not have to prove this, in order for me to know. Just like it never proved any of the above things I noted in previous chapters, until it was almost too late and I was very sick; I just knew prior to things going very wrong! Call it a sickle cell warrior's premonition, something I later found out occurs with a few other SC Warriors with sickle cell anaemia and the trait too.

I am still having to take one day at a time and just manage the pain as and when it comes, both in my body and in my head. I actually thought I was going to suffer another stroke last night, because my right arm began to tingle from my shoulder to my fingertips and my head and neck began to have stabbing pains, with severe pain in my neck. On Tuesday sixteenth February, my neck had such bad stabbing pains in it whilst I was bending my head to read my Bible during devotions, the other day. I could not lift my neck up, until my mum brought me a hot water bottle and helped me move from the seat where I was on to the sofa, where all I could do was sleep to try rid myself of the pain.

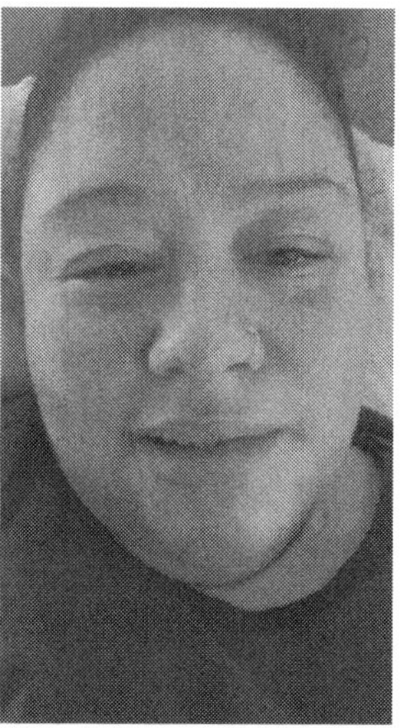

Day 1 – 17th December 2020 - first day following admission onto ward L25 - Neurology.

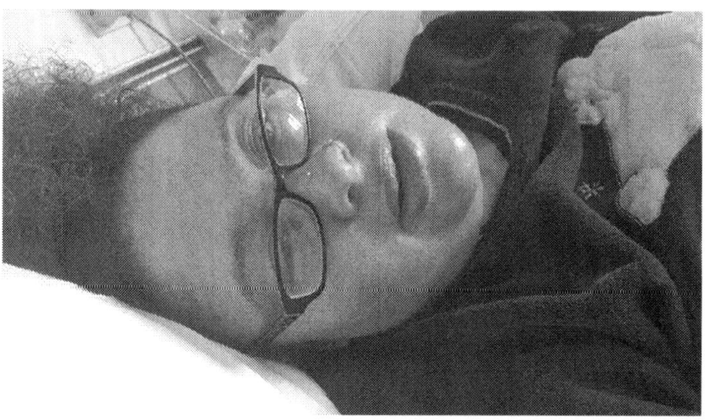

Day 2. 17th December 2020 - Exhausted and in so much pain

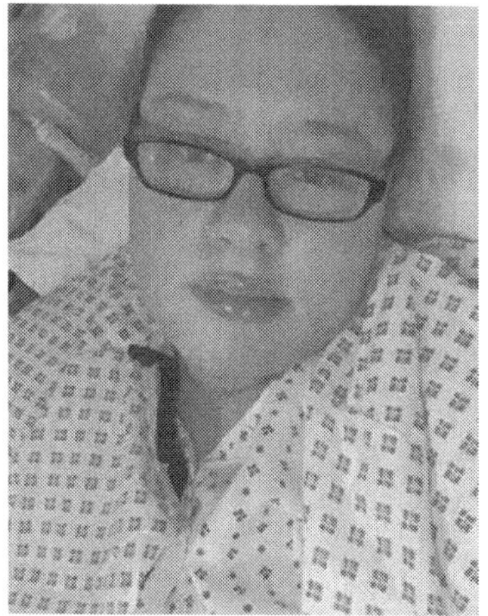

Day 3 – L25- 18th December 2020 - I could not even do my hair at this point, due to my right arm weakness and loss of strength. A lovely nurse, by the name of Maria, fought with my hair for me, despite her not knowing how to braid afro hair, despite her having mixed heritage boy children and managed to do two braids to prevent it knotting up, which I was so grateful for.

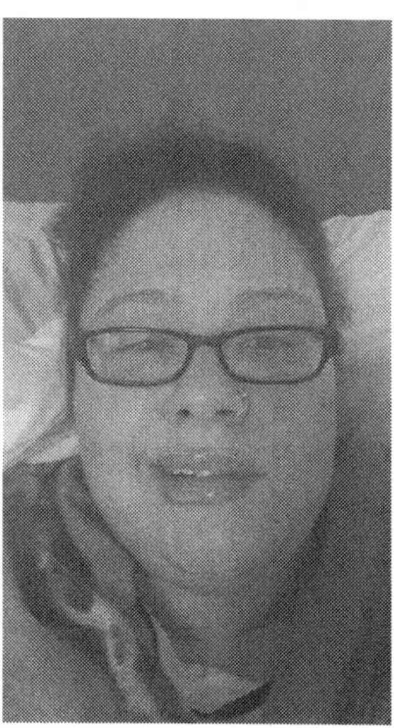

Day 4. 19th December 2020 – L25 – Unable to smile and feeling like my head was not on my shoulders and in so much pain

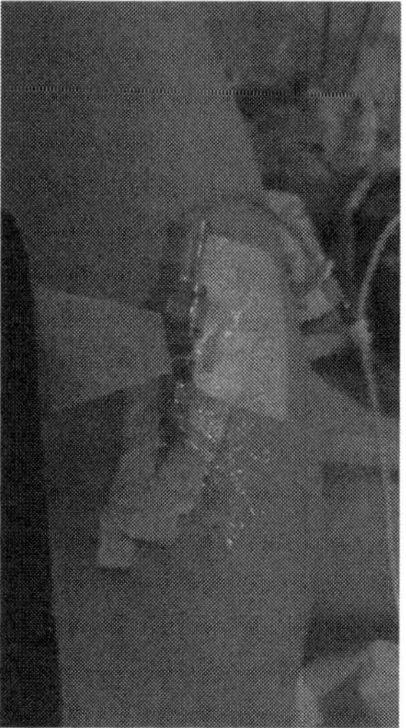

My canula – for IV fluids - I began to get afraid of needles after this admission, I have never been afraid of them before, but this was traumatic on another level.

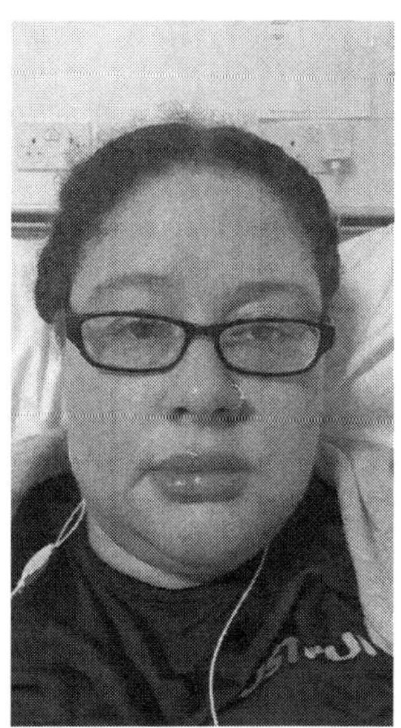

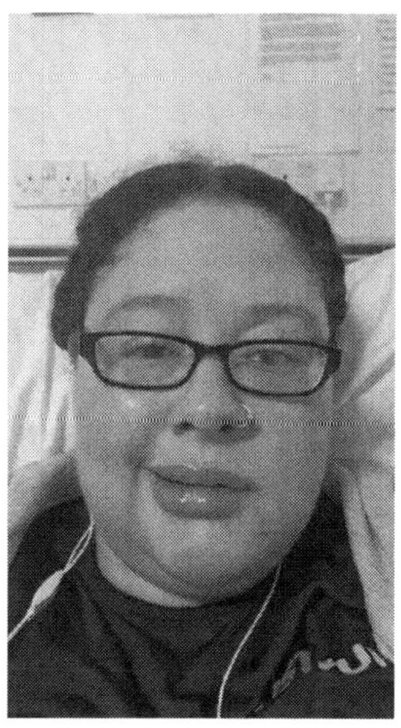

Day 8- L17 – 24th December 2020 – Discharge day

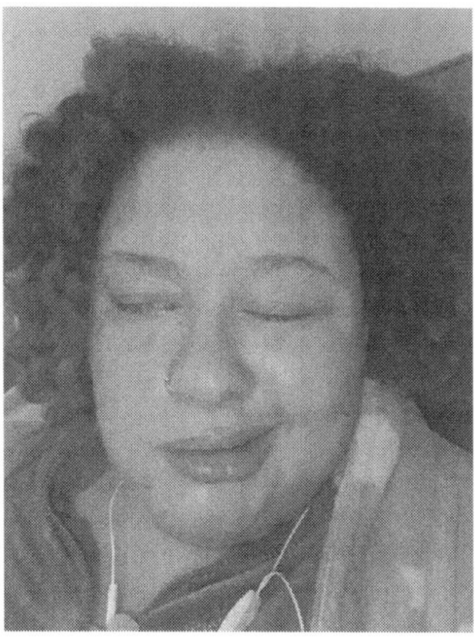

Christmas Eve - 24th December 2020 – still unable to close my eye and swollen faced or unable to smile properly

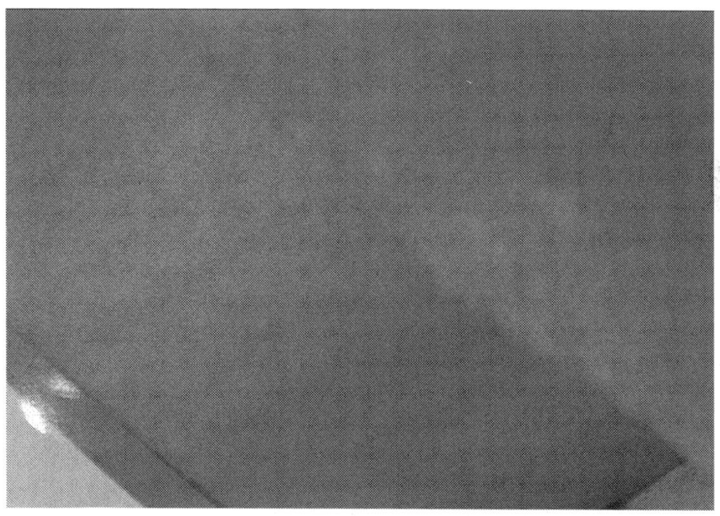

Scratches from the E.M.G. (Electromyography) test I had a few days prior to being discharged. This was done on my arms and legs and right limb weakness was confirmed.

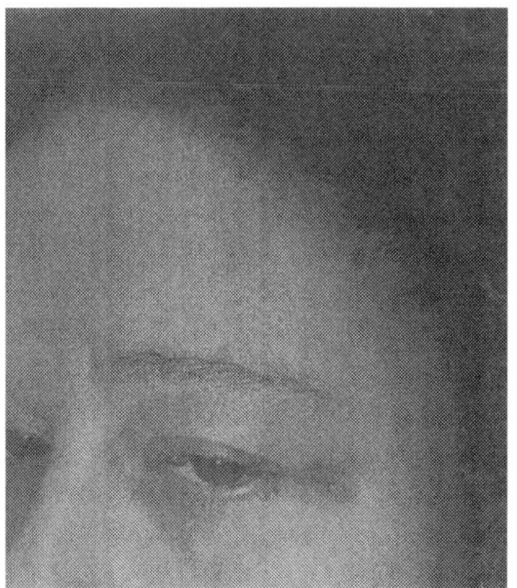

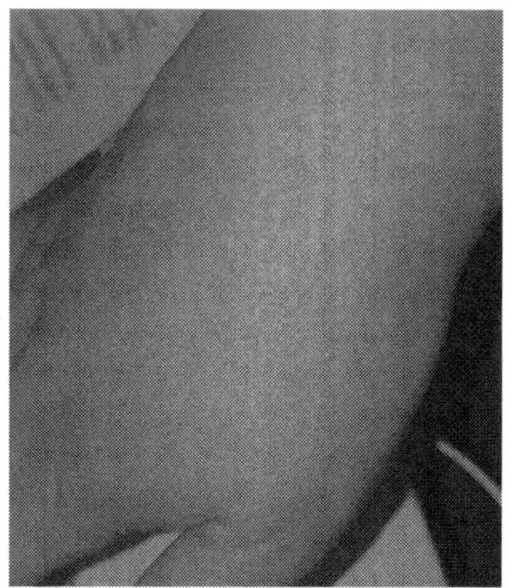

Bruising on my eye from the needle punctures and right arm swelling and scratches from the EMG tests I had done just days prior to being discharged.

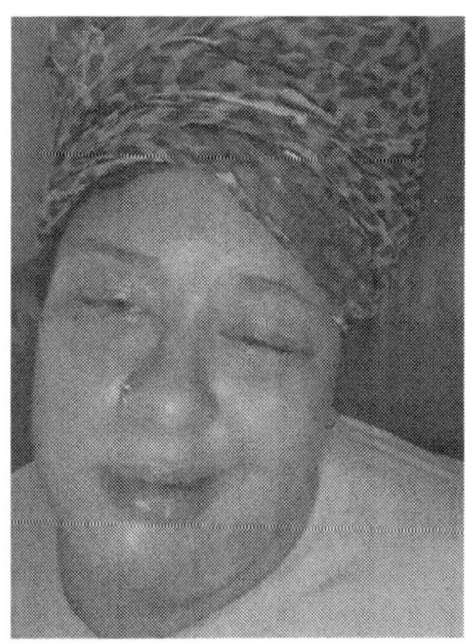

26th December 2020

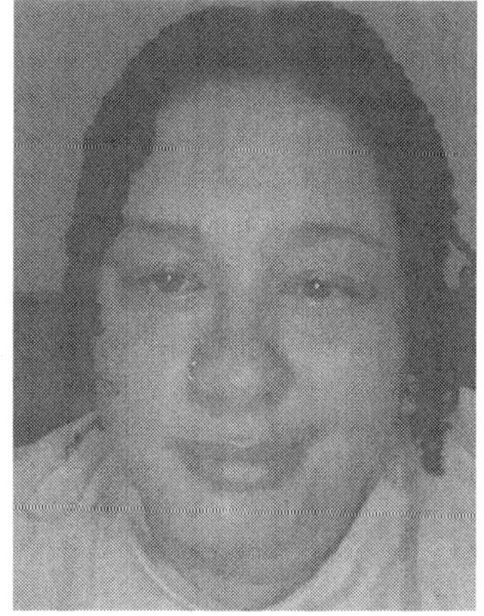

27th December 2020 – in pain, but trying to force a smile, to regain muscle function, which was much harder than it looks, it hurt my head so much.

28th December 2020 – forcing myself to utilise the muscles which were paralysed.

3rd January 2021 – swollen faced though able to smile a bit better. Eating was still difficult.

CHAPTER 13.
THINGS ARE STARTING TO MAKE SENSE: CONNECTING THE DOTS

The many sickness absences I have suffered within my working life, all now make so much more sense. Having experienced all these symptoms and so much more rolled into this past year, I now am aware of the full extent of my undiagnosed condition, despite how unrecognized it has been medically and I feel blessed to still be alive to tell my story.

I tell it not to sell a story or to depict an image of my bravery, but I feel obligated to all those silent and unrecognized warriors, out there who are 'merely' carriers of sickle cell anaemia. For those diagnosed as having sickle cell trait and are symptomatic like myself, I tell my story for them. I pray that one day their plight will be heard and that they will be given a platform and recognized as having a very real condition, a potentially life threatening one at that, when they are complaining of presenting with sickle cell symptoms.

I still have to take every day one step at a time, whilst I re-adjust both mentally and physically and try to cope with the aftermath of what has been left behind within me. The emotional side, the still ongoing pains and the uncertainty of my wait. My genetics testing has not as yet come back with any answers, but it will. I believe it will provide the doctors with the evidence that I need in order to further push for myself and it will be validated. If not, then I will continue to fight for my voice to be heard and continue my quest for others to find the support I found lacking, along with joining forces with medics in the USA, who have more experience and better expertise of treating sickle cell trait patients in crisis or with complications, even though there is still such a lack of awareness publicly and medically globally.

If it were not for my mother, who is a warrior in her own right, I would not be here today. She fights in another sense of the word, down on her knees. I am so grateful for her and for her fervent, faith filled prayers. Those fueled me up to believe I could make it through another fever filled, excruciating, painful, limb swollen night and those exhausting days where I could not sit or stand or eat by myself, but just dread the night fall and wish to God that death would just take me. The mental torture of going through such physical agony and not having help. I only went to my GP because I was working, not because I wanted to, because really, I felt they were being dismissive, as they have always been at just the mention of the words 'I have sickle cell trait' and I felt on the back of the global racial tensions that they just escalated my already heightened and distressed emotional state, which in turn did not help my crisis. I had no idea, that stress no matter what kind, was a trigger; nor did I realize that it would prove to be so detrimental to my health in every aspect of the word.

My mum's constant declaration over me was from ***Psalm 118:17*** replacing my name where I is mentioned. This caused my faith to be stirred no matter what I held on!

"I will not die, but live,
And declare the works and recount the illustrious acts of the Lord."

Psalm 118:17 (AMP)

CHAPTER 14.
SAD, BUT SO TRUE!!! MY OBSERVATIONS

It is so very sad that in order to have specific tests carried out, I had to resort to complaining. The first doctor I consulted with Dr Z, was so rude and arrogant, that I felt that it was hopeless in asking him for help, but I had to because of my workplace needing a record of this. The sheer trauma of this experience, of being fobbed off in itself, was mentally agonizing too. He said in a way that made me feel so small and angry enough to have punched him in the face, if I was physically in front of him and was in good health, "So what do you want me to do about it?" When I asked for medication due to being in the worst sickle cell crisis, as a symptomatic carrier of sickle cell and requested to have my blood tests done. This doctor was of Asian ethnic background.

The funny thing is that the second doctor I consulted with, Dr P, also Asian in ethnicity, stated that she would take my bloods, but neither my blood count nor my vitamin D levels were taken at that time. It took a further week's delay for me to have any help given. Instead, she decided to test me for sickle cell anaemia, the full-blown disease, although I had informed her clearly of my sickle cell trait status. I mean come on, after thirty-five years -- I was this age, at the onset of that severe crisis – you would think I know my body well enough, right?

I mean especially after having multiple blood tests done the year before when I had to undergo surgery under general anasthetic, which is always a clearly identified risk to the health of a person with sickle cell trait. This is one of the few acknowledged concerns to our health. You would think that the medics had performed and provided me with the right results because they had done these tests multiple times as part of my pre-operation assessments back then, which are recorded on their in-house database and on my electronic patient recording systems. I guess she did not have much faith in her own colleagues being correct, or perhaps she was a newly qualified doctor, or just purely ignorant in relation to sickle cell haemoglobinopathies, as most were, yet too proud to admit that they knew nothing about it. It is funny how admitting medical lack of knowledge, becomes priority in cases where it is life or death, many times, just to save face!

I have noted that at times, Asian doctors have either been the worst in fobbing me off or have been extremely wonderful, at the mention of a disorder--which predominantly affects black people—from African or Caribbean ethnicities--but also affects Asians too and other ethnic minority groups, including Caucasians of some Mediterranean or European backgrounds.

At times that concept of 'status' is so strange to understand, as Asians are another ethnic minority living within this country. You would hope that as fellow minorities, who do not identify as 'white in ethnicity' we would stick together, as in unity there is power, especially in cases where racial bias is at the root core of injustice! I do not care how that sounds! I am qualified, from experience, to state that very blatant fact! I am a light skinned, black African woman, who has had enough of being treated like the dirt off the bottom of someone's shoes, especially from my fellow minority, human brothers and sisters within the medical field, regardless of what their educational background or title is.

Within culture, I know, we have a status system. A colourism and class status. Status a lot of the times, is determined by the colour of one's skin. Even within our own communities, this is another thing I have grown up with experience of all too well, with being from a Southern African nation, in which Apartheid segregation was evident when my mother, who is just off-white in complexion and my medium brown skinned grandparents were growing up. The anger and hurt of this poor use of the English language and terminology, realized all too well, when my family moved over to the UK and people began calling me 'half-caste! My Aunty, who is a darker shade of brown in complexion, turned around with a look of utter shock and disgust in her eyes and shouted aloud in my mother's kitchen--which was the hub where everyone congregated to dance and eat and laugh together, in shock horror-- "Do not ever use that term again! You are not half a person!"

Half-Caste, was I later found out, an incorrectly noted derogatory term, in which the majority of 'historically uneducated', educated folks still use to this day. If only they, or you (the reader) knew where that stemmed from, in case it is a term you have ever thoughtlessly used! All I know is, I am a proud, African woman who fights her fight and knows who she is and most importantly where she comes from and my identity does not come from any human authority. It was predestined and given to me by God Almighty and as His daughter, the child of the Most High King, I am proud of what and who He made me! I hold my head high as a fighter by name!

Yes, the name '*Louise*', although I detested this when in high school, because you would hear it called out and half the school corridor would turn around in response. However, I have come to love that title, because that is what I am a '*Fierce Warrior*!' Very befitting, as '*Mwape*' my Bemba name, means '*Comfort*' or so I have been told! I will take that gladly any day, because they both are nature qualities that I one hundred percent possess!

The sad thing is, that in the past when my children died, the medical world had stuck together, despite me as their patient having recorded evidence, so now I chose to record and expose everything in great detail. Yes, I now will be recording all my conversations with medics in relation to my sickle cell status, as the flippancy in the way I have been acknowledged and treated has not gone unnoticed and lucky for them that I have only had some very near brushes with death and have won. I am grateful that I am alive to defiantly and openly fight the system!

CHAPTER 15.
EVERYDAY LIFE, AS IT IS NOW – FINDING COMFORT IN SUPPORTING OTHERS

At the moment, it seems that I have to be on high alert. My senses are more aware and my mind is more in tune with my body than it has ever been before. Although each day I have to take it as it comes, I feel ready to embrace my fight with a renewed knowledge and I guess internal strength. Perhaps this is because of my painful experiences and my current ongoing situation, as I do not feel 'normal' nor do I ever think I will ever be fully again, given the horrendous physical and mental and emotional traumas I have just recently sustained.

I feel the damage has been done medically, by them never listening and never hearing what I have had to say. I will never fully trust the medical world ever again, despite the many wonderful nurses and doctors out there who have helped me along the way. There will always be a 'nasty taste in my mouth!' I always used to hear said about one of our biggest teaching hospitals in Leeds, that 'if you want to die, go there!' I actually felt this desire to give up so deeply at one stage. I spent so many days and nights continually asking my elderly mother, 'why God had allowed me to be born'. Later on, during one of my mentally conflicting conversations aloud with my mum, she told me that 'she blamed herself for not knowing' hers or my Moroccan father's status before she got into a relationship with my father. A fact I do not believe is her fault at all. However, I do believe that she also carries sickle cell trait, as she often complained of similar stabbing joint pains and fatigue at the change of the weather, just not to the severity that I would. I later came to find out that many family members do have it, on my mother's side, but it took me allowing myself to be vulnerable and plaster it all over my social media status in the hopes to find others who were symptomatic like me to find them.

One by one people started trickling forward and flooding my inbox or texting me to say that they also suffered symptoms. Some did not even know where to begin, as testing was not standard back home, until they presented in the hospital in pain, but my experience allowed them to request further investigations and so their status was discovered.

My aim for that social media plea, was just to find someone who could understand or relate to my ongoing, mis-understood physical and mental and emotional pain. Little did I know or realize that this would be of such benefit to me and to the others around me, both here in the UK and overseas. This is when my Facebook support group for Sickle Cell Trait was born. We connected through our pain and this brought us all such relief and a renewed strength to keep on fighting our war! We have now grown from just myself and the few others who let me know their status, to over four hundred plus members. The majority of whom are symptomatic carriers or carers of someone with sickle cell trait, along with joining forces with the wider sickle cell disorder community.

Because of them bravely sharing their stories with me, I have to continue warring against the so-called medical knowledge, because there must be a reason as to why we present and with that said, I aim to find it or to connect with the right professional who will discover it on our behalf!

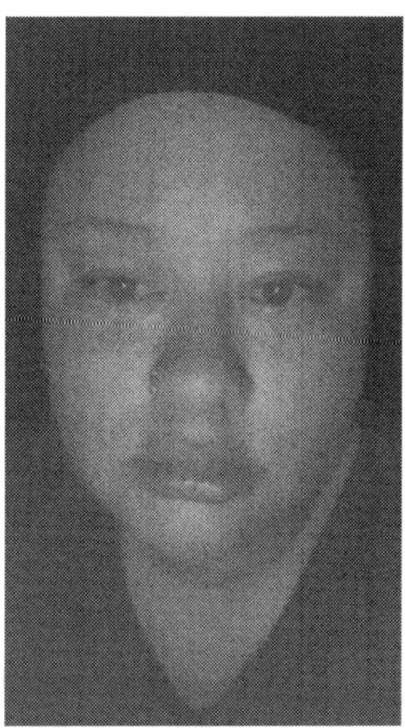

7th April 2021 – bloodshot eyes and swollen faced, these paralysing and nauseating headaches and stabbing pains on the left side are continuing to this day!

My breathing still becomes very difficult just from speaking and my face hurts so much. These headaches continue making me unable to function or sleep at night and my head feels like it is going to explode just on the left-hand side of my head. I have crisis pains on and off in my ribs, chest, arms and legs and back, along with swelling of my stomach and arm and numbness on both arms. I am still suffering with blank spells, where I totally go mentally blank and cannot remember my line of thought. My right arm continues to be weakened and although I can use it better now, I struggle doing anything requiring strength like holding a pen and writing, opening bottle lids or chopping onions if I cook, which I cannot do on a daily basis, I have to pace my body extremely well now or I cannot function at all. At times, I cannot even comb or brush my thick afro hair, so many times, I have to leave it unkempt or ask my mum, when she is well enough to braid it into two cornrows for me just to prevent it knotting up.

Due to my body still fighting to heal itself, I find I am going round and round in a vicious cycle of chronic fatigue and/or crisis pains, although much milder than they had been prior to being hospitalised along with the severe bleeding, which has lessened, but is still ongoing.

So I await my urgent hospital operation due to the heavy bleeding and clotting problem I have been having, as though my uterine lining is being shed, it appeared very thickened at my recent scan in January. My MRI for my head and on my neck was done in March 2021, yet the MRI results have still not been given to me.

I decided to telephone the genetics lab this week (seventh April 2021) to chase my results, but as per usual, I must wait until the referring consultant gets in touch with me. A wait, I feel is unnecessarily long, considering I was advised my results were sent back to the referrer at the end of February. This is the case for the majority of sickle cell trait patients, who are suffering similarly to myself. I have managed to make some progress in the urgent nature of my treatment, but this needs to happen for all of us and much quicker, because as we so often see, we only are treated when something goes drastically or dangerously wrong. My previous experiences have highlighted that, with this most recent one being the absolute worst and scariest of all my sickle cell crisis and complication experiences. How do you heal from the very real prospect of yet another close to death call, after alarm bells were rung over and over again to the medics in charge of my care.

Reality has hit, that everything I already knew and things I suspected with previous crisis experience and complications all proving to be in relation to my sickle cell trait status!

CHAPTER 16.
TRIGGERS: WHAT YOU SHOULD KNOW!

This chapter will not be huge, as I feel triggers just need bullet pointing as there are a few, however from my earlier recollections, you will notice a few of mine. Common crisis symptoms include the following;

Swelling of the hands and feet known as Hand and Foot Syndrome or Dactylitis, Fever, Sharp stabbing pain in the bony areas of the body, especially the extremities such as in the limbs, ribs, spine, but can also occur in the muscles, stomach swelling (this could indicate an enlarged spleen) and even facial swelling and jaundice, amongst a few others.

Here are the most common crisis triggers and often there is more than one particular trigger at the onset of a crisis, as seen in my experience:

- Cold weather
- Extremes changes in temperature either being too hot or too cold or exposure to either, too quickly.
- Sweating, do not allow yourself to sweat excessively and dry off quickly and change your clothing if you are working out.
- Dehydration – do not be alarmed if you drink over the recommended two litres of water a day (I sometimes drink up to five litres a day). The recommended amount is up to half your body weight in ounces of water daily.
- Over exertion – this could be physically or mentally and during exercise – let your child's school know if your child is a carrier to ensure they are aware of the extra cautions they MUST put in place.

- Lack of sufficient rest – try to have up to seven and a half to eight hours sleep a night and take naps as you need to
- Stress – try to not stress about things, physically, emotionally or mentally. Find ways to de-stress if you find yourself getting stressed out and if it is with regards to work, speak to your colleagues and your boss and advise them of the potential risk to your health. If necessary, take time off work to engage in relaxation activities and self-care.
- Surgery under general anasthetic – this is due to lack of oxygen – ENSURE your anaesthetist and doctor are aware prior to you having surgery of your trait status and ensure they provide you with sufficient blankets following surgery (the cold I felt because of lack of warm blankets being given to me after surgery, was a major trigger and caused me to be really unwell with a painful crisis and the flu for 3 weeks following my operation).
- High Altitudes – avoid climbing at altitude, due to lower oxygen levels, which is a major trigger at all times.
- Flying in unpressurised air crafts – commercial flights are usually okay for me, but I have had two bad experiences mid-flight resulting in stabbing jawbone pains.
- Infections – supplement to keep your immune system as healthy as possible.
- Whilst I personally do not take any vaccinations, such as influenza vaccinations, due to them triggering crisis for me in the past, I do not recommend that this is what you should do. Do what you would normally do, but supplement by taking additional vitamins, minerals and potent herbs where possible. Some recommended are in chapter twenty-two. I recommend consulting with a Medical Naturopath, who can help blend potent herbal tonics to aid your immune health. Please note: (I have included my Herbalist, Julia Davies contact website page in the references section of this book, should you wish to contact her for advice or wish to book a consultation with her).

CHAPTER 17.
HOW TO HELP YOURSELF AS A SYMPTOMATIC CARRIER OF SICKLE CELL

- Do Not Take No for An Answer – **push** for blood screens if you do not know what your status is – ask for a '**Haemoglobin Electrophoresis**".
- If your GP (Doctor) will not take those blood tests, ask for your full blood count, Vitamin D and folate levels to be checked.

Although a full blood count is not always reliable, as I found that my bloods had returned almost to normal by the time my doctor agreed to taking them four weeks later, mainly because I had obtained the necessary information I needed to begin building and oxygenating my haemoglobin and boosting my blood. A further four week's delay occurred due to my doctor not requesting the right tests.

- Look for your inflammation markers indication signs of infection. Complain to your surgery in writing and request for a second opinion or to speak with another practitioner urgently.
- Supplementation: If already in a crisis state, begin taking liquid Chlorophyll, Spirulina, Moringa, Vitamin B's complex, Vitamin D3, super Omega's, Zinc – these should be taken all year round every day to boost your

immune health and aid in the prevention of inflammation and to promote better health all round. **DO NOT** take Iron supplements unless okayed by your GP to prevent iron overload. Only take the above if you do not have any known allergies to the above and consult with your GP prior to taking additional supplements.

- Heat therapy e.g., warm baths with Epsom or Magnesium salts, or hot water bottles. (I use an electric blanket and a fluffy gown indoors). Layer up with thin layers, so you can remove layers if you become too warm, as being too warm can also trigger off crisis pains.
- Massage therapy aids in promoting oxygenation of the blood by getting the circulation flowing (this may not be possible depending on how much pain you are in, if already in a crisis). It may also reduce swelling of the limbs. I found this helped me following my crisis or even now if and when I am in milder states of pain and can cope with any type of touch or pressure on my body/skin.
- Hydration – your body needs more water than the average normal person without sickle cell trait. Do not be alarmed if you require more than the recommended two litres. Prior to my crisis, I was drinking up to five litres of water daily. This still continues, although mostly four litres is enough on a daily basis for me.
- Let your children's school know if they are undertaking physical activities and ensure you raise their awareness for your child's need to hydrate and therefore urinate more often.
- Rest as much as you can—due to being prone to anaemia or chronic fatigue --your body will let you know how much rest you need and let it. It is only this period of rest which will help you to heal, don't rush it. Allow your body the time it needs to recover.
- Find yourself a genetics counsellor – in Leeds, there is the Leeds Sickle Cell and Thalassaemia Service – explain that you are a carrier of sickle cell anaemia (you have the trait) and ask for help to write to your GP in order for a referral to haematology for further genetics tests to be done.

'I was informed by a genetics counsellor that there are **over fifty strains of sickle cell** (I later discovered there are so many more and some cases depending on genotype may be a form of sickle cell disease) and out of those many variants, I was informed that there are some classified as '**super sickling variants'** where carriers can present symptoms **worse than or equal to** those presented by some full-blown sickle cell patients. ***Haemoglobin (Hb) S Antilles, Hb S Oman, Hb S O-Arab*** are some of the so-called super sickling variants I was advised of. So it is worth pushing for further investigations into which variant you carry. As it all depends on the variant of sickled haemoglobin carried, as to why some trait individuals suffer, whereas others do not, hence forth the need for further research is increasingly more urgent than ever!

- Ask your GP for Mental Health counselling or advice. I found this helped me initially in trying to cope emotionally and mentally with the overwhelming fears and anxieties, which can be essentially as traumatic as the physical pain, especially when it seems too draining and emotionally exhausting for your family or carers to support you constantly. They are suffering too and may not be able to always cope, so it is good to speak to a neutral party and offload. (Whilst counselling may help initially, I found it pointless to continue having further intervention. My counsellor was very empathetic, I just felt that there was a lack of understanding on the extent and severity of sickle cell crisis pains and complications, so I found more comfort engaging in conversations with my support group, from others who fully appreciated and understood the extent of my pain.
- Medication for sleeping or anxiety may be beneficial to take. I always try to not take medication for my mental health, but it might help at times and there are herbal alternatives.
- Document everything in a Sickle Cell File known as a Care Plan – usually your doctor would do this with you, but if you are not being heard, then it may be beneficial to do this yourself. This **MUST** include all your conversations, emails to and from your doctors' practice, work etc. sick notes, hospital appointments, allergies, what supplements and pain medication you

are taking and noting what **has** worked for you. Make a note of all the therapies (e.g., heat, massage and other treatments you have used) and anything which helps take your mind off your pain, whether watching a programme or playing a game or reading a book; even writing if you are able to, although I cannot always do this due to limb swelling and severe pain).

- **Note:** how you manage your pain on a daily basis and anything you **DO NOT** consent to if you were to be taken into hospital. Carry your sickle cell file with you to any relevant hospital and GP appointments.
- **Tip**: I have begun carrying a typed-up list so that if I need to go out for any reason, instead of carrying my whole file, I can have a document of all that I am taking and all risks to my health.
- Try getting some form of mild exercise and fresh air and ensure if it's cold outside, wrap up well using thinner layers. If you find it too painful, stop. Only go at your body's own pace and intensity level and increase gradually to prevent muscle damage or crisis. Always warm up before hand and if you do train at high intensity, ensure the above along with being well hydrated. Make sure you cool down properly afterwards and rest well, as lack of rest is another trigger for crisis.
- Have a hospital bag packed and ready to go. I have begun ensuring I have a hospital bag ready for the unexpected event I need to be taken into hospital, like when I suffered my ?mini stroke. It might be handy, if ever you present in a severe crisis with complications as above mentioned within my experiences.
- **Join a support group** so that you have others going through similar experiences with you and you do not have to cope with this alone, as it can be a very lonely and isolating journey where others around you may not necessarily understand (**see my group's link in the references section of this book**).

CHAPTER 18.
EMAIL RECEIVED FROM A UK BASED SICKLE CELL CHARITY ADVISING ME ON HOW TO HELP MYSELF!

info

Tue 30/06/2020 13:32

To:

"Dear ,

Thank you for your enquiry and I am sorry about the delay in getting back to you.

I am sorry to hear about the pain that you have been experiencing.

- Here is some general information about sickle cell trait which may already be familiar to you. Sickle cell trait means you carry one copy of the sickle cell gene (HbS) and one copy of the normal haemoglobin gene (HbA).
- If you have the trait, it means your body produces a very small amount of sickle haemoglobin, which means that under certain circumstances, your red blood cells can sickle.
- Because most of the haemoglobin in your body is normal, the majority of people with the trait don't have any symptoms at all and might not even think to get themselves tested.

- Everyone SHOULD get tested because if you're a carrier (have the trait), your children could have sickle cell disease if the other parent is also a carrier.
- Being tested is also important if you're having surgery: there's a slightly higher rate of complications during surgery if you have the trait. However, if your anaesthetist knows, they can make sure you have extra oxygen, which reduces the chances of complications.
- Why oxygen? Lack of oxygen is one of the known causes of complications in people with sickle cell trait. So be careful if you're at a high altitude (e.g., at the top of a mountain, long-haul flights).
- Other known triggers are high atmospheric pressure environments (such as scuba diving) and dehydration so make sure you drink lots of water if you have the trait.
- Exercise is also a trigger. If you exercise, let your teacher/coach know you have the trait, and STAY HYDRATED.
- Complications can include pain, ruptured spleen, kidney damage.
- There is a slight risk of a rare type of kidney cancer called renal medullary carcinoma which mostly affects people with trait, but it is VERY RARE.
- There are variants of trait called haemoglobin S Antilles and haemoglobin S Oman. These show up on screening tests as sickle cell trait, but can produce symptoms similar to sickle cell disease under normal oxygen conditions. If you are experiencing severe symptoms with sickle cell trait such as frequent pain crises without flying a lot or climbing mountains or getting dehydrated, ask to be tested for haemoglobin S Antilles and haemoglobin S Oman: they need a further lab test.
- As I am sure you have seen, most research and leaflets/info online suggests the trait rarely carries any symptoms. However, we are gaining a picture that the trait can cause pain in a number of individuals. For those with sickle cell trait, 20-40% of the haemoglobin is HbS (in comparison to 80-100% in patients with a sickle cell disorder), suggesting that some sickling and the associated joint/crisis pain can occur.
- It would be useful for you to ask your GP for a referral to a Sickle Cell and Thalassaemia Centre or to a haematologist for further insight into your symptoms and ask for the further

screening tests listed above. You can also ask to be re-tested in case you have sickle cell disorder rather than the trait.

- I am aware that you have tried to contact your GP and had no luck there, but it may be worth persisting with them. You can try and ask your local sickle cell and Thalassaemia centre in Leeds to see if they can carry out the blood test if the GP is not forthcoming.
- In order to minimise further pain, I will provide you with some of the advice I give to individuals living with a sickle cell disorder which may be helpful.

Folic acid is good for stimulating the production of red blood cells and improving anaemia. Try taking folic acid supplements, and eating foods rich in folic acid e.g., leafy green vegetables (broccoli, kale, spinach, peas), dried beans, and almond milk. B-12 vitamin is also necessary for the production of red blood cells in the bone marrow.

- Foods rich in B12 vitamins include fish, beef, lamb, cheese and eggs. These foods can help to increase haemoglobin levels. It is also important that you remain hydrated, stay warm (minimising any draughts in the house) and do your best to stay relaxed as stress can cause crisis pain.

If you would like to read more into sickle cell trait, please click on the links below which explain situations where you need to take care.
https://patient.info/health/sickle-cell-disease-sickle-cell-anaemia/sickle-cell-trait
https://www.cdc.gov/ncbddd/sicklecell/toolkit.html
You may be interested in the article below about sickle cell trait from Metro news.
https://metro.co.uk/2019/09/16/isnt-enough-awareness-sickle-cell-trait-problem- 10751779/
If you do have severe pains that isn't eased by taking painkillers, I would advise you to seek urgent medical advice.
I hope some of this information is useful to you.

Best wishes,"

CHAPTER 19.
MY INITIAL EMAIL TO A UK BASED SICKLE CELL CHARITY REQUESTING FURTHER ADVICE

From: Enquiry [redacted]
Sent: 19 June 2020 15:18
To: Info [redacted]
Subject: Sickle Cell [redacted] Enquiry

You have a new enquiry with the following information:

Name: [redacted]
Email: [redacted]
Location: Leeds
Message: "Hi, I am a 35 year old half Zambian half Moroccan woman with SC trait living in Leeds. However, ever since moving to the UK as a 5-year-old child with my family from South Africa, I have suffered with painful Crises mostly during winter, or also during summer, or after travelling, which became less frequent as I got older. However, travelling by plane has begun causing me severe pain as I am getting older. Neighbours who had SC disorder and frequent hospital admissions and losses in their families through

SCD always told me I have it too, as I would experience the same symptoms of pain as they would without the severity and other complications, but am prone to infections often falling quite ill such as pneumonia and kidney infections and I have a weak immune system. I had not suffered a painful crisis in a couple of years as I have always taken necessary precautions, until having an operation in November and despite saying how cold I was following this and explaining how it affects me, to no avail and then this Tuesday 15/6/20 where I struggled to breathe following cardio exercise and felt quite lethargic and emotionally exhausted due to the current climate and racial tensions globally! Later Tuesday night I began having a fever and my right forearm and fingers swelled and were so sore to even gently touch my skin, with stabbing pains in my bones, which spread into my legs and my spine and upper back. My stomach hurts like it is cold inside and tender and I've slept so much as I feel so weak. I drink up to 4 litres of water daily and I'm continually wrapped up warm and feel even slight breezes in summertime. I do take over the counter painkillers, but as I have managed these symptoms for years and lived with them ever since I can remember and after having 2 children who didn't survive after premature birth and complications and being so sickly myself I've had visits on occasion from the Leeds sickle cell service, am just wondering is there anything else I should do to help recovery please, is it normal for a trait carrier to be in pain for so long or to be so sensitive to the cold? I have had to rely on my mum to even hold a knife to eat or to type on my behalf as bending my joints is so painful. GP's have never listened to me, which could have proved fatal on occasion and when I attended A&E prior to being admitted twice I was told I could have gone into a coma. I know it is rare to suffer with just carrying SC Trait, but have also spoken to my university lecturer and read experiences from those with SC Trait who have suffered through their lives like I have and just would like further advice please on how to help myself and to educate others who don't understand it. Many thanks"

CHAPTER 20.
LETTER RECEIVED FROM A SICKLE CELL & THALASSAEMIA GENETICS COUNSELLOR TO MY GP

Hospital

LEEDS

Direct Line:
Fax:
email:
Date: 7th July 2020

Dr
The

Dear Doctor

Re
NHS No
DOB

" I had a telephone consultation with the above patient on 2.7.20, who was advised by sickle cell society to contact the sickle cell team at Leeds.

She told me that she is a carrier of sickle cell. She gives history of pain crises over the years, which appear similar to sickle cell disease and the recent crises was on 15.6.20. She states that the swelling of arms has come down, but she is still having tenderness in arms, legs, ribs and hips. She is taking codeine as prescribed by yourself which she feels is making her more tired, but it is not reducing the pain. She stated that she had migraines and throbbing headaches earlier this year and she was referred to the neurologist, but nothing came out of it due to covid-19

She demonstrates good knowledge of genetic re sickle cell condition via contacting professionals and reading several research articles.

There are three are different strains of sickle cell including haemoglobin S Antilles and haemoglobin S Oman. These types are described as super sickling haemoglobin variants, whose carriers express the abnormal haemoglobin at

between 40-50% (R L Nigel, S Daar et al). We have previously thought that the trait rarely carries any symptoms, however we are gaining a picture that the trait can cause pain in a number of individuals for those with sickle cell trait where 20-40% of haemoglobin is HbS (as compared to 80-100% in patient with sickle cell disease)

█████ expressed her anxiety and fears regarding her health and having all the symptoms similar to those who have the disease and wants more investigations to find treatment.

Considering her history of symptoms/pain crises and her anxiety I believe it will be useful for her to have further tests to determine the variants of sickle cell such as Hb S Antilles and HG S Oman and also a referral to Haematologist for further insight into her symptoms.

I will be grateful if you could kindly consider arranging blood tests and referring █████ to Haematology for further investigations to determine the cause of her symptoms. "

Kindest regards

█████

Genetic Counsellor

Sickle & Cell Thalassaemia Team

CHAPTER 21.
MY NEWFOUND MISSION

Going through this awfully challenging year, has almost broken me. My head at present is only able to focus on one thing at a time. I currently feel so exhausted much of the day, every day, no matter what I do. However, I am utilizing self-help tools and focusing on one goal per day. This at times involves signing up for free webinars with like-minded individuals, be it other sickle cell warriors, or people who have had something to overcome in life and hearing their stories once they have made it through. Other times, it means engaging in motivational speakers' challenges. The one I just took part in was the Tony Robbins; New Year, New You Challenge and I pushed myself hard to attempt to get out of my comfort zone, in the knowledge of growth being uncomfortable and painful.

Nothing ever comes out of being comfortable, except staying stagnant and I needed to keep moving so that I continued to grow! So, I fought with my mind, against my inner reservations and joined. Mostly because I felt so stuck and I felt helpless and I felt that if I did not do something, then I would sink into the lowest chasm of depression and having fought my way out many times years ago, I did not desire to venture back there again!

I am still fighting this physical, mental and emotional battle, as it was a huge physical war, it will take a little time to get over and move forward completely. This does not mean I am dwelling on the past, it just means I am human and I have been through a lot, although this last year was the most mentally challenging and reality shaking experience I have ever gone through in my life.

I mean how do you cope with being told there's nothing physiologically wrong with you and tests disprove what you are saying, yet your body is not functioning normally, or it is acting up in such a debilitating way and you are physically and mentally left scarred and in a crippled state? That's the most difficult challenge; fighting a mostly hidden battle to the world, yet feeling like you are dying inside, because your own body's attacking you!

So due to all the above, I did that challenge and it helped solidify what I knew I MUST do. As Tony Robbins says, "If you can't, you MUST!" I have always known I am supposed to publicly speak. Well, I had not been engaging with my support group doing Facebook lives, prior to this challenge. Instead, I chose the easier options of pre-recording videos and posting them, but now I know I must get uncomfortable and speak live, so I can engage from my heart and relay a non-scripted message out to all those who need to hear it and be encouraged through it! I hope that my story does that and gives hope to all those out there who are in need of it, or those who feel alone or who experience the medically unexplainable, because that is my aim!

Expressing myself and allowing others to see me at my most physically, ugly and vulnerable state has been extremely difficult, but it is not about me! As I have just found out, this cause so close to my heart is so much bigger than just me, so I choose to no longer hide myself away due to embarrassment of what I look like when I am not at my best, but rather I choose to share myself with the world, determined to make a difference by helping others know that they are not alone!

These experiences are what in actual fact have made me, well ME! These traumas collectively, although sad and extremely painful at the time I was going through them, I am now at peace with and these very things have built my character and driven me to a point in which I am well equipped to fight this battle with even more determination and focus than ever before! So now I embrace the past and look ahead to the future and am so grateful to still be alive and to have an amazing family and a great support group and for these very personal experiences, which have more than qualified me to assist the medical world and seek out answers!

"For if you remain silent at this time, liberation and rescue will arise for the Jews *[SCT warriors]* ***from another place, and you and your father's house will perish [since you did not help when you had the chance]. And who knows whether you have attained royalty*** *[a platform]* ***for such a time as this [and for this very purpose]?"***

Esther 4:14 (AMP)

Note: I add ***SCT warriors*** and ***a platform*** in the text when I am praying this declaration over my life with regards to the situation I am currently going through.
This is what I do with all scriptural based prayers! I felt this is the very purpose of my experiences, to assist in urgently speaking out against injustices we as sickle cell trait warriors experience because of being ignored!

The time is NOW! I am called for 'SUCH A TIME AS THIS!'

CHAPTER 22.
MY DAILY HEALTH SUPPLEMENTS AND RECOMMENDATIONS

Here are the supplements which I take on a daily basis, in order to build up my immune system and keep my body and my red blood cells at optimum health, to the best of my ability. I have provided you with a brief overview of what each supplement's health benefits are.

Although not an exhaustive list of every supplement I have been taking or herbal teas I am drinking, these are my everyday MUST HAVE's!

Should you wish to purchase any of them, I have provided the **link** to my **affiliate websites**, where you can **register** and receive a **discounted** price from the quoted retail price. The web shop links are situated within the reference section of this book.

Liquid Chlorophyll

Chlorophyll is the life blood of plants. Characterised by its green colour and flavoured with natural peppermint to give it a refreshing taste. Drinking liquid chlorophyll helps oxygenize and cleanse the blood, making it an all-around blood cleanser and aids in alkalization and hydration of the cells along with helping to build haemoglobin levels.

£15.25 RRP

Vitamin B Complex

Containing an array of B Vitamins, including Vitamin B12 which aids in reducing tiredness and fatigue, whilst nourishing the nervous system and boosting cognitive function. Riboflavin (B2) helps the body metabolize iron and promotes healthy vision, skin and helps maintain healthy red blood cells. Vitamin B6 helps regulate hormones and promotes good glycogen metabolism.

£13.45 GBP

Vitamin D3

Vitamin D is known as the sunshine vitamin, due to it's overall health boosting benefits. It helps support the immune system, lifts the mood and aids in promotion of healthy teeth, bones, joint and muscle development and function.

£19.95GBP

Magnesium and Calcium Combo

These two vital minerals depend on each other for optimum absorption into the body. Whilst calcium contributes to promoting of healthy bones, teeth, muscles and aids in neurotransmissions. Calcium also is an essential component of blood clotting and helps with digestion.

Magnesium helps over 300 bodily enzymes start up and helps contribute to the health of bones, teeth and muscles, preventing cramping, reducing tiredness and fatigue.

£16.45 GBP

Zinc

An antioxidising mineral, essential for overall immune health. It helps with reducing free radical damage of the cells, aids in cognitive function, helps maintain healthy hair, skin and bones and aids in promoting good vision. It is also great for normal fertility and promotes a healthy and normal reproductive system, along with aiding in tissue and wound healing.

£9.95GBP

Pea Protein Plus

A cruciferous vegetable sourced protein blend. Free from gluten, dairy, lactose, saturated fat and cholesterol. This nutritious blend contains a blend of multivitamins including B vitamins to combat tiredness and fatigue, as B vitamins cannot be stored in the body, so require a top up daily. Filled with superfoods such as spirulina and chlorella and an array of anti-oxidant rich fruits and vegetables, this blend can be used in conjunction with a healthy diet, as part of your daily supplement intake, or as a filling meal replacement. Each serving of 30g contains 13g of vegetable protein and high in super omega's from flaxseeds.

£24.95GBP

Take the _Free_ Lifestyle Analysis Questionnaire

All the body's key systems are interlinked, therefore when one of these systems is out of sync, it will ultimately result in the body being out of balance and cause you to become unwell. Why not take the free lifestyle analysis to find out which of your body's key systems requires a boost. This questionnaire was developed by experts in the field and designed to assist you in highlighting which of your bodys systems requires a nutritional boost to restore balance to your body. The ***link*** to this affiliate page is provided in the ***website recommendations*** at the back of this book.

ClenZ

A powerful nutritional powerhouse, suitable for daily use. You may read up additional information regarding any of the below individual ingredients, from the websites referenced at the back of this book. Key ingredients consist of the below:

Moringa Olifeira – this nutritional powerhouse and superfood contains Vitamins A, B, C, D and E and folic acid. It also is full of over 92 nutrients and 46 different antioxidants, basically great for many bodily functions, oxidation, blood cleansing and alkalising.

Pineapple – This fruit is great as an anti-inflammatory, is immune building, contains digestive enzymes and is rich in antioxidants.

Nettle – This bitter plant acts as a blood cleanser and anti-inflammatory. It aids in lowering blood pressure and helps regulate blood sugar. Nettle contains all the essential amino acids, Vitamins A, C, K and several B Vitamins, minerals and fatty acids. It also relieves arthritic inflammation.

Dandelion – This root plant may be looked upon as a weed in general; nutritionally and in herbal medicine, dandelion is revered as a potent remedy for many ailments. It assists in lowering cholesterol and blood pressure, aids in the regulation of blood sugar, fights inflammation, is antioxidant rich, promotes healthy liver function and may aid in fighting cancer. Dandelions contain vitamins A, C, K, E and folates and some B vitamins.

Peppermint – Peppermint helps freshening breath because of it's anti-bacterial properties. It contains menthol, which increases better blood flow and is cooling thus it can aid in relieving tension headaches and migraines. It is found to increase energy; eases digestive discomfort and flatulence by relaxing the digestive system. Because peppermint is antiviral, anti-inflammatory and anti-bacterial it can aid in relieving clogged sinuses, minimise allergies and can also aid in the relief of painful menstruation cramps, due to being a muscle relaxant. Peppermint is also a good tea to promote good sleep, due to being caffeine free and again as mentioned above, having muscle relaxing properties.

Fenugreek – This herb is a great multi-purpose ingredient used in Indian cooking. It can be taken as a supplement or used in alternative medicine. Some of it's benefits include helping to lower blood sugar levels, therefore great for diabetes. It aids in reducing cholesterol and can help suppress the appetite. Due to it's anti-inflammatory properties, it can aid in reducing inflammation and some studies have shown it's benefits in treating ulcerative colitis. A pilot study also discovered that it can be used to treat heartburn, with it's effects being similar to antacid medications.

Psyllium – This is a type of fibre which acts as a gentle laxative. It absorbs water in the gut, as it is a soluble fibre, which the body cannot fully absorb, which aids in promoting healthy bowel movement. This in turn assists in lowering blood pressure and aids in regulating cholesterol levels and blood sugar and due to it's prebiotic nature, it supports good intestinal health. Psyllium is also a good supplement for the pancreas and for maintaining a healthy heart, because of it's cholesterol lowering properties.

Prune – Prunes are high in fibre, which aids in healthy bowel movement; is high in potassium, which supports digestion and regulates blood pressure, aiding in the promotion of good heart health. This also helps to promote healthy nerve impulses and muscular contractions. Prunes are high in antioxidants and help reduce inflammation and aids in keeping bones healthy.

£39.99 RRP

CHAPTER 23.
POETRY – MY PAIN RELEASE

Mummy's Little Angel

Dedicated to my perfect little angel baby Judah Ziyoni!

When I looked into your angel face,
My eyes filled with tears;
And all the pain that I had been through,
Dissolved with all my fears!
The joy that flooded my inner being,
At having you all to me!
This beautiful baby for the first time I was seeing,
Now meant the world to me!
The delicacy of your baby soft skin,
The helplessness of your tiny frail frame,
Made me quiver inside;
The way you would need to depend on me,
Filled me with such pride!
The beauty of your innocence,
The thought of you and me;
The realization of you being mine,
The knowledge of me being your mummy!
You can't imagine how I felt to hold you in my arms,
To keep you with me as close as could be;
Without having to give you to anyone,
The way I felt so calm!
But now, how the pain fills my heart and soul,
Because of the fact that you're gone!
I knew I'd have to let go somehow,
Just didn't know what was in store.
The thought of finally saying goodbye;
Of having to officially close my heart's door,
Never really entered my mind;
Mainly because I had a hope of you coming home,
I guess, as they say, because love is blind!
I waited for so long for you,

And now that you're finally here;
Seems like I'm lost despite what I went through!
I've come too far to turn back now,
To learn to love you, but then to lose you!
I know that one day we'll meet again,
But that doesn't make the hurt go away;
I'm still alive and I have to go on,
But for now my little angel;
Your mummy loves you and won't forget you,
And I'm looking forward to seeing you again,
Someday!

Written by Louise Rachael Mwape Miller – 8th July 2002
© 2021 Louise Rachael Mwape Miller

Amazing Grace

In loving memory of Josiah Azaniah Hakim – my 2nd angel baby

Lord I thank you for your Amazing Grace,
That brought this baby to me!
This tiny little angelic being,
I'll hold in my heart eternally!
I praise you for who you are,
The Great I Am indeed!
For you and only you,
Could create so perfectly!
From his fingertips, to his tiny little toes,
And the eyelids;
Though tightly closed,
To his perfectly formed, distinct nose!
The glossy skin, so like velvet to touch,
Now, how I miss him so much!
My baby boy,
A source of joy;
But now a sweet memory!
When I think of all his organs formed,
The breath you let me see;
For two hours and fifteen minutes,
That tiny life you shared with me!
Though tears may fall and I sometimes feel sad,
At him not being with me,
My heart is truly free;
For through this precious little child,
A new beginning you've given me!
I thank you for friends and family,
Who have sojourned here with me!
With an open mind and a willing heart,
I'm ready for the healing to begin;
For it's your love and grace that's carried me,
And filled me with peace, abundantly within!
Now I'm ready to embrace my destiny in you,
As in my weakness;
You're my strength,

And in the darkness;
You're the light that carries me through!
I thank you for your Amazing Grace;
That's allowed me bid a final goodbye,
For its only through you as my sufficiency,
Giving me grace to release him back to you!
My loan, he was,
Though brief it was;
He's at peace at home now,
In the sky!
Though my love for my little boy lingers in the atmosphere,
Will never ever die;
It's your Amazing Grace travelling with me,
I'll thank and praise you;
For you reign on high!

Written 4-5th March 2008
© 2021 Louise Rachael Mwape Miller

Forever Valentine

Dedicated to my future husband, from a heart filled with love!

Baby will you be mine,
Not just because today is Valentine!
I want to spend an eternity with you,
Sharing my whole life with you is all I want to do!
I'm in love so deep,
It's like a dream that lasts forever,
Picturing you and I,
Having fun together!
The things we'll do and say,
To enjoy being with each other;
The way I feel good inside,
Because you're the sweetest lover!
I feel the love that's in your heart and mind,
When we talk on the phone;
Wishing and waiting,
Till we can spend time together,
All alone!
It seems like an age to me;
To have to wait for you,
But you see baby it just shows;
My love is pure and true!
So, when you get the chance;
Don't hesitate to call,
Because one day I'll have the chance to love you,
With me, My all!
The way I'll love you, nobody can,
Because I do it perfectly
The way my being glows with pride,
Because you're the one for me!
So, I promise you baby, you'll hear me cry for joy;
The day you blow my mind!
The way my heart will beat for you,
So intimate and divine;
If you promise me,

You'll always be,
My Forever Valentine!

Written – 5th February 2004
© 2021 Louise Rachael Mwape Miller

2020

A heartfelt tribute to the year I will never ever forget!

2020 You've been so good to Me,
In hindsight, made me see;
How change and a reset was necessary,
To develop and rebirth individually!
You Started off like any other year,
Then the whole world was gripped by fear;
Of this scary chasm of disease unknown,
Sent us all panicking, whilst being stuck at home!
Hospitals filled up to their brim,
Worldwide things began looking and feeling so grim!
Lockdown, flights grounded, plenty jobs have been lost.
Black lives brutalized, no matter the cost!
George Floyd murdered on international TV!
Rayshard Brooks, Daniel Prude, Breonna Taylor;
Philando Castille to name just a few.
Their names etched, scarred forever in the hearts of our society;
Divide and conquer seemed to be the tool!
Those racist police minority,
Full of evil seemed to prevail at the world's core;
Not realizing what was yet for us in store!
Covid-19 was just the surface given distraction,
When deep down control seemed to be the main course of action!
Of the new world order dictating to the masses;
No vaccination, so no free passes;
To life as we knew it just not so long ago,
Although it seems like a lifetime has passed!
Many have died, but not just from this!
When they've recovered it seems that victory is missed!
Myself, I went through the worst sickle cell crisis;
But it has made me realize just what my fight is!
A warrior was reborn from deep within my soul,
My trauma and pain connected me to others;
Who collectively suffer just like I do!
Rare renal medullary cancer, headaches, pain crisis!

Silent strokes, sight loss and carers who feel helpless,
Because sickle cell trait is deemed healthy!
Yet here we are; over 150 of us have found each other!
From all corners of the world we united,
Our number growing as warriors;
To raise awareness and bring about change,
To how sickle cell disorder from the medical world is accessed!
Hopefully more research and funds will be raised;
So that this new year 2021 can bring new hope,
Not just for us,
But for the whole globe!
2020 just when I thought I'd gone through the worst,
You decided to show me just who you are!
It ended with me being hospitalized,
Mini stroke; query Bell's Palsy they say!
They're not sure, so it remains to discover,
But I'm a fighter, so at home I recover;
And will turn what you brought to destroy me
Into my testimony!
2020 by God's grace, we still stand,
And the majority of us will take each other by the hand!
You've shown us greed and selfishness
And the ugliness of being hu-man;
But you've also shown us strength, love, unity,
Joy and pain which brings forth beauty!
For in our losses, we have learned to find,
A resolve that can only be God sent;
To rebuild and reset and more so count what truly matters;
Through the challenges we've individually,
And collectively faced,
You've taught us to embrace,
A deeper and more meaningful outlook,
And aim even higher than before;
Knowing that there are no boundaries once we set our minds to it!
Whatever our goals are;
They're attainable,
Because of You!

Not letting go of our immense determination;
To find joint solutions
And rebuild
Our nations!
So, as we say goodbye to 2020,
At midnight tonight;
Here's wishing you all a Happy, prosperous
And God-filled New Year!
May it be your best yet,
Come what may!
2021 Welcome!
And let us not forget,
From where we've come from;
So that we don't become stagnant,
But continue to grow;
And become better,
For each other.
And learn to humble ourselves,
Before our creator;
Because humanity has become so arrogant!
That's our fatal flaw,
Whether you agree or not!
I wish you all a very happy, peaceful and reflective
New Year,
May it bring out the fighter in You!
I've learned a lot;
And for that I'm personally grateful;
Especially realizing that my God,
Is always faithful!
No matter how much pain I've been
Mentally, emotionally or physically in,
He's helped me make it to the other side.
My rainbow in the rain is the fact that I am
Still alive!
So finally, without looking back
I thank you 2020 for all the chaos
You've caused;

Because without you,
I wouldn't be able to give a round of applause,
To all who deserve a little recognition!
Y'all friends and family,
Know just who you are!
Thank you for making it this far,
With me!
God bless, I love you and
I pray the best of 2021
Over and for you in Jesus name!
Happy New Year 2021!!!

Written 31st December 2020
© 2021 Louise Rachael Mwape Miller

END

REFERENCES

Get in touch and follow me on social media

Instagram: @mwapemiller or @jemozainnerbeauty
Facebook: @mwapemiller or @jemozawellbeing
Twitter: @jemozawellbeing
YouTube: Mwape Miller
https://www.youtube.com/results?search_query=mwape+miller

Books

Sickle Cell Natural Healing: A Mother's Journey; Tamika Moseley; Author House; 2013
The Comprehensive Guide to Nature's Sunshine Products; Horne and Balas et. Al; 6th Ed. Tree of Light; 2014
A Life With Sickle Cell Anaemia; Dr David Owoeye; KDP; 2020
Staying Alive in Toxic Times; Dr Jenny Goodman; 2nd Ed.; Yellow Kite; 2021

Local Services

The Sickle Cell Society UK
54 Station Road
London
NW10 4UA
Email: info@sicklecellsociety.org
Tel: 0208 961 7795
www.sicklecellsociety.org

Sickle Cell and Thalassaemia Genetics Counselling service Leeds
www.leedscommunityhealthcare.nhs.uk/sicklecell

The UK Thalassaemia Society
www.ukts.org
Tel: 0208 882 0011

The UK National Screening Committee
www.screening.nhs.uk

Facebook Support Groups

Facebook Sickle Cell Trait Support and Information Group-Global Voices United

https://www.facebook.com/SickleCellTraitSupportandInformationGroup

Sickle Cell Group Australia – Australian Sickle Cell Advocacy

https://www.facebook.com/australiansicklecell

Sickle Cell Trait Journal

https://www.facebook.com/groups/sicklecelltraitjournal

Book an appointment with Dr Maisha M.D.

https://www.nscrxption.co

Websites for further information and supplementation:

https://www.mwapemiller.com
https://lilyandloafinternational.com/?aff=408775
https://lilyandloafinternational.com/products/liquid-chlorophyll?aff=408775
https://lilyandloafinternational.com/products/vitamin-b-complex?aff=408775
https://lilyandloafinternational.com/products/vitamin-d3-high-strength-vegan?aff=408775
https://lilyandloafinternational.com/products/calcium-magnesium?aff=408775
https://lilyandloafinternational.com/products/zinc?aff=408775
https://lilyandloafinternational.com/products/pea-protein-plus?aff=408775
https://lilyandloafinternational.com/pages/lifestyle-analysis?aff=408775
https://shopbydesign.com/TSLife/#/shop/detail/SUP20-UK/from/84167

Book a Consultation with Julia Davies - Medical Herbalist

https://www.juliaherbalist.co.uk/

Websites of Reference:

www.cdc.gov>documents

www.ncbi.nlm.nih.gov/books/NBK537130/Factsheet_sickle_cell_trait.pdf
https://www.facebook.com/notes/104083161471437/
https://www.cdc.gov/ncbddd/sicklecell/traits/html
https://www.asonefoundation.org/
https://wdconsct.org/
https://www.youtube.com/watch?v=OGT0Vn8QRSM
https://www.youtube.com/watch?v=EIkq1ZePjEk
https://www.ncbi.nlm.nih.gov/books/NBK537130/
https://sicklecellanemianews.com/2021/02/04/abnormal-flow-sickled-cells-damages-blood-vessels-supercomputer-comet/??utm_medium=desktop-push-notification&utm_source=Notifications&utm_campaign=OneSignal
https://twitter.com/sicklecell101/status/1360293686781743104?s=19
https://youtu.be/lwrKB_cU_tM
https://m.youtube.com/watch?v=J0KNUsrZBcQ&feature=share
Https://ashpublications.org/hematology/article/2020/1/562/474283/Optimizing-the-management-of-chronic-pain-in?searchresult=1
https://sicklecellanemianews.com/2021/01/20/being-productive-during-crisis/?utm_source=Sickle+Cell+Anemia+Ne
https://twitter.com/RMCAwareness/status/557968076088827904?s=19
https://patient.info/treatment-medication/living-with-a-long-term-condition
https://aussicklecelladvocacy.org
https://sicklecellanemianews.com/2020/10/23/how-manage-sickle-cell-crisis-home-tips/?cn-reloaded=1
https://www.theguardian.com/society/2018/jul/19/husbands-stroke-showed-best-worst-nhs
https://www.hopkinsmedicine.org/news/media/releases/er_doctors_commonly_miss_more_strokes_among_women_minorities_and_younger_patients
https://www.memorialcare.org/blog/mini-strokes-time-brain
https://www.womenshealth.gov./a-z-topics/sickle-cell-disease
https://twitter.com/DrBryantLeyva/status/133599367835905?s=19
www.oralee.org
https://www.sicklecellsociety.org/resource/massage-therapy-treatment-management-sickle-cell-anaemia/
https://www.reuters.com/article/uk-sicklecell-brain-

idUSTRE64A5M420100511
https://youtu.be/Hnxqc4sT851
https://www.bbc.co.uk/news/uk-england-stroke-staffordshire-50955190
https://www.sicklecellsociety.org/wp-content/uploads/2018/05/EMPLOYMENT-SICKLE-CELL-ANAEMIA-HANDOUT.pdf
https://www.gov.uk/definition-of-disability-under-equality-act-2010
https://www.healthline.com/nutrition/6-benefits-of-moringa-oleifera
https://www.healthline.com/nutrition/benefits-of-pineapple
https://www.healthline.com/nutrition/stinging-nettle
https://www.healthline.com/nutrition/dandelion-benefits
https://www.healthline.com/nutrition/peppermint-tea
https://www.healthline.com/nutrition/fenugreek
https://www.healthline.com/health/psyllium-health-benefits
https://www.healthline.com/nutrition/benefits-of-plums-prunes

Register for Blood Donations

https://www.blood.co.uk/why-give-blood/demand-for-different-blood-types/black-asian-and-minority-ethnic-communities/#:~:text=Thalassaemia%20and%20sickle%20cell,-Thalassaemia%20mainly%20affects&text=Patients%20with%20these%20disorders%20need,still%20become%20a%20blood%20donor.

ADDITIONAL THANK YOU'S

To my Angel babies who both had to die in order for me to begin the first steps towards this fight, little did I know it back then! I will always love you and continue to celebrate your precious little lives! Thank you for giving me the courage to speak out!

To Aunty Zeb, who was as kind and understanding to me as Mrs. Juma used to be when she used to visit me at home all those many years ago when I would suffer crisis. Thank you for going out of your way to help me and to listen. You were the first person other than my mother to make me feel heard and acknowledged that my pain was very real! A real angel on earth! God Bless you!

To Deb for being so kind to me and referring me to Zeb and for understanding my misunderstood, painful state. Thank you for being an amazing friend and colleague!

To my beautiful and intelligent, super smart and funny niece Kayla for all your love and laughter through it all! You truly are God's gift to me my precious, angel girl! Thank you for giving me such joy despite all the pain! The poise in which you handled seeing my deformed face and you still loved me anyway, even without knowing whether it would stay like that or not, it really moved my heart! You are so caring and express such maturity and an understanding beyond your years! You're Aunty Lulu's baby my boo boo! I love you with all my heart! You mean everything to me!

To my brother Naeem for being our support bubble and stepping up and helping us when I could not! Thank you for being there for mummy when I was in hospital and for seeing how in need I truly was, even when I was too proud to ask! I could not ask for more in a brother and a friend than I have had in you from when you were born. You were the first baby I was privileged to love and I am grateful that you got my back 'bruv'! I love you from the depth of my heart!

To my girl Fifi for your love and care for me whilst I was physically unable to do anything much for myself. Thank you for hearing my pain and being there and learning about my condition and really being there for mum and I considering lockdown restrictions. We love you always boo!

To ba Mayo Bakalamba, my beautiful Aunty Mary! I am forever grateful to you for loving me. Despite our differences and despite the arguments and all the in-betweens, you've been my second mama from birth, the one I could call to talk to and pray with when mummy or me were so severely sick! Thank you for the concern I heard in your voice, because you could not be physically present, but you were here in spirit! I love you more than you will ever know!

To Aunty Maxine for being such a gift and a prayerful support and uplifting me. The daily messages of encouragement knowing that someone was praying for me, regardless of the pain of grief you were battling yourself, you still found and continue to find the strength to give of yourself to me! Thank you for my hospital lounging gifts too. I love you!

To Pauline for your kindness in instructing me on what to do next, even though I was not your patient. Thank you for listening to me and not dismissing me from a professional healthcare perspective. Thank you for guiding me and helping me to prepare myself for the unforeseen hospital admission. Because of you I was ready, when the time came!

To my beautiful and super caring Baji Misbah! Baji, I have no words to describe how grateful I am to you for the many times you have been there for me. Thank you for listening to me hours on end and visiting me, albeit socially distanced at my doorstep to drop off goodies or essentials to me. Thank you for being my courier back and forth when I was in hospital and my connection between home and my mum when she was too vulnerable to come herself. You truly are my sister from 'anova mista'! I love you more than words can express baji!

To my beautiful sister Fouzia- I am beyond grateful for your support and love and sisterhood babes, no matter how much you were going through personally, you still had time to check on me! I will be forever grateful to you sis always. Thank you for keeping me informed of life beyond me, so I had something other than my pain to dwell on. I appreciate you and love you from the bottom of my heart!

To Ken, thank you for checking how I was daily, despite the turbulent year we had. I appreciate your care and your love. I will forever be grateful to you for everything! Filled with so much love from the bottom of my heart!

To my baby sis Masego, thank you girl for loving me and encouraging me and helping me hold on to the Lord! Thank you for praying with me and being there for me! Thank you for sharing your heart with me! I love you more than words can ever express sis!

To Jamila and Mel – my sisters. Distance and Time may separate us, but when we get together it has always been and always will be love! I love you both from the depths of my soul! Jamila my birthday twin, thank you for being my bestest friend since Primary school sis! I am honoured and grateful that you have been in my life all these years! Thank you for your wisdom and your love! I love you sis and owe you so very much for you have travelled some of the most turbulent times of my life with me and never judged me, nor did you question any of my frequent last minute cancellations. Now you know the reasons why!

To Aunty Jackie Brown, ('JackJack') – my beautiful Aunty-Mummy! Words can never begin to express the treasure I have in you! You mothered me and nurtured me and loved me as your own! Thank you for brightening my days and for the laughter filled nights, when my skies were so dull and grey! Thank you for clothing me, when I could not clothe myself. I love you and Josiah had the best other Grandma in you!

To my niece Gladys aka 'Shanu' (My little light) - I love you and am so grateful for your life! Thank you for standing on the word of God and hearing me when my no one else heard my voice, you immediately rose and called for action in 'prayer'! I appreciate you so much!

A very special shout out to Phostina, mwaiche wandi thank you for being my little warrior sister. Though our pain connected us, I appreciate that our faith and passion for spreading awareness in the hopes that we can find answers to our many unanswered questions, keeps us going together full steam ahead! Thank you for being a part of my personal journey and lifting me up when I feel I cannot go on alone. Thank you for making me feel I am never alone as a symptomatic carrier sis and for your encouragement. I thank you for your love sis and I love you my fellow Zambian sis! I am here to lighten your load, as you always lighten mine! We will find the help we desperately seek sis, thank you for lending your voice and your pictures for the website use, for the bigger picture!

To my fellow sickle cell trait warriors who are symptomatic like me (my Facebook virtual support group – Sickle Cell Trait Support and Information Group – Global Voices United), too numerous to shout out in here, but you know who you are. I am especially grateful for you! Because you were searching, we found each other! I thank and salute you for not giving up on looking! You will never understand how much it meant to me when you began requesting access to the group one by one! The relief I felt at hearing similar stories to mine! The unified pain we have suffered, but because we did not fit the generic box, we have had to suffer disconnected from medical aid or support and the indescribable many traumas we have endured because of it! I am grateful that you found me when you did.

Your stories soothed my soul, because I lived them too! The times I felt I was losing my mind, just hearing from you would give me the will to continue in this fight! Thank you from the bottom of my heart! This story is for all of you and all others in our sickle cell trait family who have not had the ability to find us yet! May this reach all corners of the earth and encourage you to know that you are not alone and may this give you the strength to fight! I stand with you!

Ba Agnes – sis thank you for putting SCT on the radar of Australian Sickle Cell Advocacy's (ASCA) talks (Sickle Cell Talks with Agnes on Facebook). You inspire me so much with the great work you are doing!

To all my fellow sickle cell warriors (full blown), who have recognized me as a sister warrior in my own right. The years I have fought isolated and alone, but I am so grateful to be finally heard. Special thanks goes to Chanel Taylor (**@unsicklemycells** – Instagram – please follow her page all and Sarah Jane Nkrumah – Instagram - **@sicklecellunite**). My sisters, thank you so much for being such an inspiration in showing me that our pain has purpose and for believing me when I first approached you both individually. I was so scared to voice out that I was a carrier of the trait, who suffered, for fear that my pain would be questioned because I knew and understood your pain, yet I felt that I had no right to speak up, due to being told I did not suffer anything in comparison to you and I could not bear that from fellow warriors within our SC community, but you opened your hearts to me, despite your pain and trauma and you checked on me and reached out to me too! I appreciate the work that you do in raising awareness about SCD and have so much respect, love and admiration for you my fellow Warrior Queens! Blessings always! Together we stand unified by our common SC Disorders battle and I know we will make a change across the spectrum of sickled haemoglobinopathy disorders!

To Aunty Jenny, my Mary Kay mummy and confidant! Thank you for loving me as your own and making me laugh always! Your belief in me and tunnel vision kept me focusing on the destination and outcomes always, despite how ill I was. I will always love and treasure you and looking forward to more fun times together when the madness is over!

To Ba Geraldine, Gabriel and John. I am so grateful to you, my amazing family that you kept me grounded during the most difficult times. Thank you for your encouragement and love. I appreciate you all so much and am grateful to know that my family lifted me in prayers across the waters. I look forward to the day we live closer by each other! SA here we come!

To Mr. P (aka Patrick), words can never express just how much you mean to me! From day one way back then man, you had my back. Thank you for being more than my friend, you have been my big bro, my homie, my confidant, my protector! Through our ups and downs in life, the pain, the tears, it will always be nothing, but love, thank you for not judging me when I'm sick!

To Simon, for all the times you have picked me up and been such an amazing friend! Thank you for being an anchor and mediator in the good times and the bad! Thank you for bringing Gertrude into my life and being my family! I love you both and my niece and nephew!

To mummy Hazel, thank you for loving me despite the distances between. The Lord knows you were and continue to be an inspiration to me, as a strong, black Queen. Your love and friendship kept me during the hidden battles I faced, whilst a student in Manchester. I love you with all of my heart, light and blessings always – out of sight, but never out of mind! Much love to Iman and Rachel always.

To my big and small Aunties, my mum's sisters Regi, Aunty Lena, Aunty Mabel and Aunty Angela, Ba Mayo bakalamba ba Aunty Gracie, thank you for calling when you found out what happened! Despite the physical distance between us all, it helped me find the strength to fight, thank you for showing us just how much you care! I love you my Aunties so much!

To the wonderful church congregation of BICC Cottingley, thank you all for loving mum and I so much and for providing your help, when we were unable to provide for ourselves. You were truly a God-send at our most vulnerable stage of this fight. Thank you for checking on, shopping for and praying for both mummy and I. We truly cannot express our love and appreciation to you enough! May the Lord continue to bless and keep you all!

To Aunty Icilma and Uncle Addison for listening to the voice of God and calling at just the right time to keep me sane and pray for mum and I when she almost slipped away! I appreciate you and love you and thank you for looking after us in the ways you did and continue to do always! Thank you for standing with and fighting on our behalf too!

To Toyin, thank you sis for being there when I needed someone the most! I will never forget your kindness and love! I love you always girl!

To Drew, thanks bro for lending a helping hand, praying for and with us and for being family, we appreciate and love you!

Thanks to Ronald, Chido and Charles for being there for Naeem, mum and I when we went through some of these traumatic times together! We appreciate and love you guys!

To 'Miss Sunshine' AKA Aunty Patricia (Pat)! I will never forget! I treasure our beautiful times and recall such precious memories! Judah Ziyoni would have had a second mum in you. There is no one else I would have shared him with! I love you – my 'woman of colour!'

To Sharon for being a friend and keeping me company through text, when it felt my mind was slipping away and I was sinking into depths of despair so deep, I could not control it! Thank you for the sweet gifts of flowers and bath bomb, I so desperately needed a soak following my hospital admission when the reality hit and I began to sink so low! Thank you for no added pressure to text back or to talk work! The de-stress and disconnection was and is necessary and appreciated as I continue to recover!

Thank you to my baby bro, my cousin Cox, who called me via video call from Zambia just to check up on me daily until you had no phone. I love you and miss you and am grateful we are family!

To my cousin Alister, our 'family doctor' thanks Cuz for bringing people to the group and sharing awareness of this very desperate and essential cause! I love you and am so grateful you are my cousin/big bro! Words can never express just how much you mean to me!

To my sister always and my beautiful baby cuzzie, Ruby, I love you mama so much! You are my baby sister forever and you were my rock when I needed you the most and your love got me through losing my baby boy! Thank you for your love and your heart! I treasure our relationship and friendship always cuz! Grateful that although we are cousins, you were the best friend I could have ever asked for, within my family!

To my sisters Kathryn and Donna, thank you for the wisdom, the steadfastness and the encouragement and most of all, your love! No matter what timeframe or distance between us, thank you for never taking it in any way except, I have been dealing and going through life's battles, as we all do. Thank you for always allowing us to pick up from where we left off – to me that is the real meaning of true friendship, sharing and loving no matter what or how long it has been! I love you and am always here for you too and I remain forever blessed to have such amazing and inspirational big sisters! May the Lord continue to use you and bless your lives to enrich others as you have so done mine! Kathryn thank you for inspiring and nurturing my broken heart through my loss and loving me through my trauma waaay back then when I was too young to understand any of it!

To Aunty Jackie C, thank you for checking in on me and encouraging and uplifting me. I am so grateful to have you in my life and thank you for the years of praying for me. I love you and will forever uphold you in my prayers!

To my incredibly huge Family, far too many to individually name. both near – Dave - thank you for believing in me cuz; Kenneth – I miss you cuz; Arthur - I'm grateful we have finally met and are close now, after all these years! To my family abroad - I love you all and am grateful for all of you who cared enough to call and check on me and mum, when I could not find the strength at all to even talk! I appreciate you all and hope to God that we one day meet again whilst still on this earth! Grandpa left us such a great legacy, 23 children and beyond!

To Uncle Patrick and Ba Cordie, words cannot express just how grateful I am to you both for your love and kindness! We are so grateful that we got the chance to see you both before the whole world went crazy, thank you so very much! We love you!

To Danielle, thank you for sharing with me your journey and checking in on mine! Sisters for life, neighbours once upon a lifetime, to our memories of everyday growing up back in Chapeltown! Lots of love to you and Jean always!

To Aunty Jeannie – words can never express just how much I love you! Thank you for caring for mum and I through some of these most difficult journeys mentioned in my life! I'm truly grateful to the Lord for you and love you with all my heart!

To my sisi Debs, thank you ma De for loving me and being the best big sister ever! That bond can never be broken no matter what! Despite you not understanding sickle cell trait patients being symptomatic, thank you for being there through my illnesses because of it. No matter how different things are now, thank you for being my sisi through my ups and downs always, remembering the days of the frizz sistahs always and forever! Love you so much more than you'll ever know!

To D, you will never know just how much you push me and continue to inspire me to do better and become more than what I am! Thank you for always challenging me to be my best and making me think outside the box when I am at my lowest points! I appreciate your friendship and the love and will never, ever forget! To answer your observation --I see my value in helping myself by helping others and I have you to thank for that!

Thank you to all my friends who have in some way input their love and poured kindness on me, whilst I was at my most vulnerable and in my choosing to share my most private moments. Thank you for no judgments and thank you for listening (the ones of you who really showed your care). I will forever be amazed at those of you who went out of your way to check on me and shower me with such love! I appreciate and love you! Usha, Anu, Crystal Douglas, Vanessa, Aissata, – words can never ever begin to express the love I have for you beauties! Thank you for the beautiful and special times my sisters! I cannot begin to even express my gratitude to you from the depths of my heart!

To our family from our Chapeltown days, Aunty Ita, Aunty Judith, Uncle Irvin, Aunty Sylvia, Aunty Ajibike, Aunty Carol, Aunty Arlene, Uncle Owen and Aunty Joyce, Aunty Joyce B, we owe you all so much! Thank you for being there for me and mum always and for praying more than I've ever known people can pray and teaching us how to pray too! We love you all so much! The bond goes beyond words! Thank you Aunty Ita, for always remembering my pain and for praying me through it! Thank you Uncle Irvin for looking after Naeem and I and for always being there for us! You were like a dad to us growing up and for that I'm forever grateful! Your family will always be family to us, Aunty Naomi S, I love you! I always looked up to you back then when I was a child! Mr Derrick, thank you for your counsel and being the best mentor ever whilst I was so shy at school and timid, as a young black woman, who had been through so much and with so much naivety and had nowhere to seek counsel within church that I trusted. I am grateful you took me under your wing! I'm forever grateful to you!

To my foundation family from day one, my Aunties and Uncles, Aunty Kalenga, Aunty Mayizhi, ba yama ba Matthew, Uncle Zac, Aunty Naomi, Aunty Tuli, Aunty Tembi, Aunty Keone and Uncle Shupikai, Aunty Lorraine, Aunty Ema, Aunty Margaret, Aunty Rosebud, Aunty Agnes, Aunty Gladys, Aunty Rebecca M. Aunty Shabnam - There are so many things I am grateful to each one of you individually for! You were our family from the day we first met and the bond will never ever die. Thank you for carrying us when we were broken, crying with us when we needed a shoulder to cry on. Thank you for loving us when we felt empty and praying for us when we needed uplifting, feeding us when we were hungry and giving us a drink when we were thirsty (literally) and laughing with us through it all!

Aunty Jeannie, thank you for being my confidant and always opening your doors so often when I was growing up and listening to my heart, when I was so confused, with all I'd gone through. I miss your old house and ours too, because it was easy to just wander to you and catch up while you were busy cooking or baking in the kitchen. '*Natasha sana bonse mukwai for everything! Kya leboha! Ngiyabonga gakulu! Tatenda sikulu! Zikomo kwambiri! Thank you*!'

To my fam; my day one's Esther, Elijah, Naledi, NJ, Kezia, Aongola, Victoria, Tanga, Thembi and Mzi, Liz, Lydia, Josh - I love you all so very much! No matter how much time passes between, I can never ever forget how much we have each shared together! Khaleda (boro boyn), Juna, Khairiah - my high school besties! My baby siblings, my older siblings, thank you for being there for me each and every step of the way! The memories within this book and all those painful experiences I recalled during the writing of this, I owe so much to you all, thank you for believing in me and loving me through my silence during many of these episodes! Thank you for the multitude of good times too, but I am ever so grateful that I had you in my corner during every single stage of my life you were either individually or collectively a part of!

To my boss, thank you Vanessa, for being a caring and understanding manager. I appreciate your understanding and concern for what I have been going through for far too long now! I truly was happy being part of your team, when I could function normally!

To Tony and Sage Robbins, Team Tony and KK, thank you for helping me find some form of clarity in the foggy mental state I was in and am still battling through. Although I began writing this last year, I appreciate you for helping me turn my old story into an empowering healing journey enough to see it through to finish with the momentum your NWNY Challenge provided me with. Despite the physical and mental challenges, you helped me to overcome and keep getting up daily! I will be forever grateful to you. You are incredible and I hope one day I will get the chance to share my story personally with you! Blessings and love always you beautiful people!

To NWNY Challenge's- Step Up Squad – Angel – thank you for being such an inspiring leader to create a group which inspires others to step into their best selves through this Tony Robbins challenge! You are a beautiful human being and I love the person you are! You make my heart smile and I am so grateful that this journey connected me with you! Thank you to all the inspiring individuals out there within the NWNY Step Up Squad, love hearing and seeing your progress and knowing just how far we each have come in our individual journeys! Proud of you all!

To Tadeja, thank you for choosing to share your journey of how to begin and the next steps with me and spurring me on to become greater than ever before! You inspired me to keep writing and helped my excitement levels knowing that no matter what this is going to help somebody else out there! Thank you for your friendship and your motivating messages and the way you helped me focus solely on my vision of helping so many other people and spreading awareness of this awful condition I am fighting! I am so grateful to have had you to be accountable to, even for a little while! I look forward to one day meeting you in person and not just on a video call, so I can give you a big hug and say "*We did it despite all our challenges*!"!

To Sandy, cuz we have always had such fun and giggles. Thank you for the conversations and the years where I could call you to just chat and no matter what I was going through, you never judged me! I appreciate the person that you are and am so grateful that yet again, through this NWNY Challenge, we were able to hold each other up to fight another day! Thank you for your encouragement and love and belief in me, you make me smile especially when it is really hard! I love you cuz and I am so proud of you! I cannot wait until you reach your end goal and beyond! This is just the beginning of the best chapter cuz, despite the pain!

To Julia, my medical herbalist - thank you for hearing my urgent plea and helping me to treat myself naturally with your expert knowledge of nourishing the body from within herbally. Your knowledge, patience to provide both my mum and myself each with carefully blended bespoke tonics to boost our immune health and to provide the nutrients we desperately needed, when our health was in desperate need of medical intervention. When no medic listened, you did and I am so grateful to you for your intervention at the time we found you, I love my bespoke tea and my Gingko tonic, it is helping me with my brain fog immensely, even though I am still going through my healing process!

To all the medical professionals willing to listen to our stories, undertake further research and lend a helping hand in bringing about change! We appreciate you and all you do!

My utmost thanks to Dr Tomia Wooten-Austin, Dr Kim Smith-Whitley and Dr Maisha Pasante for the time you are taking to spread awareness and help medics and the public understand and undertake further research into this very real condition. Thank you for "treating the patient and not just the symptoms" as Dr Maisha stated during the informative and very educational webinar I attended recently regarding sickle cell trait. May the narrative out there be updated and may all community surgery staff be re-educated so that they can do better for the ones who access healthcare in desperate need of help! Thank you – your work will save more sickle cell trait warrior's lives!

Lastly, I'm grateful because I cannot believe I managed to complete this book, let alone start it whilst I was feeling so unwell and actually make sense whilst going through all of the above challenging experiences, I'm grateful for my ability to fight. I am grateful for my stubbornness and drive no matter what pains I go through! Thank you Lord for making me this way!

TRIBUTE TO MY GRANDPARENTS

MR AND MRS J.W. MILLER

Ba Shikulu and ba Mbuya wandi!
The best Grandpa and Granny anyone could ever have!
Thank you for leaving such a legacy behind in the strength of us Millers, no matter what we go through!

My baby brother and I
South Africa 1989

The young family – Chapeltown
England 1990

ABOUT THE AUTHOR

Born Louise Rachael Mwape Miller, 21st November 1984 to Zambian Mother, Maggie and Moroccan Father in the United Kingdom. Known as Lulu or Mwape to her family and close friends. Her mother had travelled to England and later moved there, long before Louise was born. Shortly, after Louise was born her mother returned to her homeland of Zambia and later settled in Swaziland (now the Kingdom of Eswatini), where Louise's brother Naeem was born, before they finally settled in South Africa. Louise's early life was spent roaming in the beautiful outdoors and playing happily in the parks of Johannesburg or at the beach in Durban, with her younger brother Naeem.

When Louise was aged five years old, Louise's mother brought her young family over to the United Kingdom, where she hoped to bring her children up and build a life of opportunity for them, as England was always where she had hoped to settle when she had children. Louise now resides in Leeds, UK with her mother, brother Naeem and twelve-year-old niece Kayla. She achieved her NVQ level two in Business Administration at College in 2003. Later she went on to become one of the first nationally recognised band four, Associate Practitioner's within a clinical histopathology laboratory in 2009 – 2011 whilst studying for a healthcare science degree in Manchester. She then relocated back to Leeds in 2012.

Louise later began running her own Holistic Health and Wellbeing Business including non-surgical Aesthetics from 2015-2017 after completing a Level two Nutrition Advisor course and an ITEC Level three certification in Massage and Complementary Therapies.

She also combined this with the completion of her Level three Personal Training certificate, as a fitness and wellbeing fanatic herself, until her health began to drastically deteriorate due to her Sickle Cell Trait status.

She has had to close her business and has been working for the National Health Service, as an administrator ever since.

Printed in Great Britain
by Amazon